An Angel Told Me So

Wilma Jean Jones
Michael McAdams

BALBOA.
PRESS
A DIVISION OF HAY HOUSE

Balboa Press books may be ordered through booksellers or by contacting:

Balboa Press
A Division of Hay House
1663 Liberty Drive
Bloomington, IN 47403
www.balboapress.com
1 (877) 407-4847

Because of the dynamic nature of the Internet, any web addresses or links contained in this book may have changed since publication and may no longer be valid. The views expressed in this work are solely those of the author and do not necessarily reflect the views of the publisher, and the publisher hereby disclaims any responsibility for them.

The author of this book does not dispense medical advice or prescribe the use of any technique as a form of treatment for physical, emotional, or medical problems without the advice of a physician, either directly or indirectly. The intent of the author is only to offer information of a general nature to help you in your quest for emotional and spiritual well-being. In the event you use any of the information in this book for yourself, which is your constitutional right, the author and the publisher assume no responsibility for your actions.

Any people depicted in stock imagery provided by Thinkstock are models, and such images are being used for illustrative purposes only.
Certain stock imagery © Thinkstock.

Printed in the USA.

ISBN: 978-1-5043-8603-6 (sc)
ISBN: 978-1-5043-8604-3 (e)

Library of Congress Control Number: 2017913032

Balboa Press rev. date: 05/01/2018

An Angel Told Me So

An amazing collection of messages
and teachings dictated directly from
spirit teachers/ angels
through Wilma Jean Jones.

Dictated in first person
with many of the messages and
teachings signed by the spirit teachers
presenting this information.

But how do you know this to be true?

An Angel Told Me So.

VOLUME ONE

About the Cover

There have been numerous stories and accounts of feather crowns being found in the pillows of loved ones who have crossed over. It is said that upon the passing of a devout child of God a crown would be found. This is an older story as feather pillows were commonly used during the period where accounts of these crowns have been reported. Wilma Jean Jones' mother, Mary Culbertson, was brought up in the Pentecostal church. A devout Christian, Mary was called to the ministry when she was 30 years old. Mary received sermons and words to songs given through her by divine inspiration on numerous occasions. Mary had been diagnosed with sugar diabetes and was required to take insulin shots for years. As she continued to get worse she was taken to a hospital in Columbus, Ohio in September of 1950. Lying in her hospital bed with tears in her eyes she prayed to Jesus to heal her of her illness. She reported seeing a vision of Jesus appear in her room and the words to a song began to come into her mind. She picked up paper and pencil and took down the words as they were given. That night she was healed of sugar diabetes and for the rest of her life would never again take an insulin shot.

Upon Mary Culbertson's passing in 1964, Wilma Jean kept the feather pillow that her mother Mary had slept on. She placed this pillow in a plastic bag and kept it on a shelf in the closet of her bedroom. Wilma Jean said that one day while working in her kitchen she heard a voice say "If you look in the pillow you'll find a crown." Wilma by this time had become accustomed to receiving messages and teachings with words dictated to her mind in her sessions but hearing this voice was a new experience. She did not hesitate. She stopped what she was doing, went to her bedroom and took the pillow down from her closet. She cut the end of the pillow open and gently reached inside. In this pillow Wilma Jean found the promised crown pictured on the cover. She would never have known it was there if not for the voice that spoke to her that day.

About the Author

Wilma Jean Jones

Wilma Jean Jones is a devout Christian and a daily reader of her Bible. Wilma feels she has been spoken to and advised throughout her life regarding spiritual matters. In 1977 Wilma was led to sit down and receive messages and teaching dictated directly from spirit teachers/angels in dedicated sessions. Little did she realize at the time that these messages and teachings would continue to be received for twenty two years. Wilma had always been open to spiritual leadings and was prayerful in seeking protection and guidance from God as she received these writings. When Wilma was led to receive she would sit down at her typewriter, light a candle, and say a prayer asking for protection. As the words from spirit teachers/angels were given Wilma would actually "see" these words appear in her mind three and four at a time. Once these words were typed they would fade away and three or four more would appear. This is the manner in which these messages and teachings were received.

Working with her son Michael this collection of messages and teachings are recorded in three volumes of her book *An Angel Told Me So.*

About the Author

Michael McAdams

Michael McAdams has felt a sense of destiny and purpose his entire life. A life long sincere seeker of truth, Michael has endeavored to reach out with an open mind to all sources available. Brought up in the Pentecostal church, Michael's uncle was a fiery Pentecostal preacher by the name of John W. Sullivan. Although Michael has always felt more spiritual than religious, communication from the highest possible source has been his goal as he enables his mind to receive information and direction that allows him to help the greatest number of people. "When the student is ready a teacher will appear" has been very appropriate for Michael as his path has consistently brought him together with individuals, books, and sources of learning that have allowed continued growth and spiritual enlightenment. One of Michael's preferred books in addition to the Bible is the Urantia Book. Michael offers a set of his own writings called Spiritual Parchment Prints available on his website spiritspeaks.com.

An Angel Told Me So

An amazing collection of messages and
teachings received over a twenty two year period.

Dictated word for word.

Received and recorded by
Wilma Jean Jones

Dedication

To my daughters, Marsha and Jamie
For all their love and support.

And to my son Michael
For his love, loyalty, and devotion.

Wilma Jean Jones

Prologue

When the words started to come I wasn't afraid. I had been spoken to before. Not necessarily spoken to with a voice I would recognize, but spoken to in thought directed to my mind. I have on occasion been spoken to with a voice but that is rare. THAT will really get your attention. I knew what I was being given was meant for me. It was so appropriate for what I was going through at the time that I knew these spirit teachers/angels had access to information about me that no one else could know. How could they know my thoughts and feelings so well? How could they describe in such detail and with such depth what I was going through and dealing with? I couldn't let this pass without taking notes. The more I wrote down the more I received. These spirit teachers/angels complimented me for my willingness to be receptive and were grateful for my efforts in recording this information. I started setting aside time to be able to receive these messages and teachings and believed it was important to record and save these messages and teachings in written form. I started using an electric typewriter to receive these messages and it was remarkable the teachings that were given for me and for others, namely my son Michael who had supported me in this effort and for whom I also received personal messages and teachings.

Initially I started receiving what I would refer to as general teaching messages. These messages and teachings are relevant to most all who would read this information. As I continued to receive and take down these messages I began receiving more specific information addressed both to me and my son Michael pertaining to what we were going through and experiencing at this time in our lives. The depth and quality of these messages and teachings were amazing to me. Many times these spirit teachers/angels would use words that I was unfamiliar with and I would look them up in the dictionary after the message had been received to confirm their meaning.

I would become involved in a divorce and it was a rough time dealing with the mind set of someone who turned out not to be the person you thought you knew. These messages began to prepare me not only for what I was to go through in this process but to give me insight into the mindset of the man that I would eventually no longer be married to. These messages contained information as well as prophecy about what would transpire and I was amazed at the depth, detail, and accuracy concerning what did indeed turn out to come true.

I started receiving personal messages in the same session for myself and for my son Michael as he was not only extremely interested in these messages and teachings but also very supportive in this endeavor and work I was doing. Many of these sessions in which I received messages for both myself and Michael would sometimes take three to four hours. As I was led to receive these messages I was already prepared with my typewriter set up in a quiet area of my home. I would light a candle, say a prayer asking for protection, and insert a blank sheet of paper into my typewriter. I would date the paper, drop down five lines and indent just as you would do to write a letter. As I relaxed I would see in my mind three or four words that I would take down. As soon as the last word was typed those words would fade away and three or four more words would appear. This is the manner in which these messages were received. Many of the messages were addressed specifically to me and my son Michael. Others were offered as what I would refer to as general teachings.

Three extremely amazing occurrences would become apparent to me as I received and recorded these dictated messages and teachings. Many of the sentences given in these messages are over one hundred words long with punctuation. They are not run on sentences but given with a depth and quality that contains so much information that they must sometimes be read numerous times just to get the full meaning of the information and teachings being conveyed.

Another interesting note was these spirit teachers/angels knew how much paper I had. Repeatedly on single spaced full page messages they would place the last word in the bottom right hand corner of the paper so tight there was only room left to add the period. How could you do that? Many times I was so focused on taking down the words exactly as they were being given I was not even aware I had reached the bottom of the paper until the sheet of paper popped out as I hit the return button.

Additionally, of the over two hundred twenty five single spaced typed pages of dictated messages and teachings received, many of these messages are signed by the name of the spirit teacher or teachers who presented this information. This was not given so much as a hand written signature but as a name presented at the end of the message. On rare occasions I did see a hand written signature and I duplicated it to the best of my ability.

To this day I am in awe at the depth and quality of the information given in these messages and teachings and the sheer number of messages received over this twenty two year period. Even though many of these messages were given as personal messages for me and my son Michael, and many more are given as general teachings, everyone who has read these messages have said they felt a personal connection with this material. It's as if these messages and teachings have been woven with a universal thread that resonates with those who have the opportunity to read this material. A personal chord appears to be touched with the readers as if these spirit teachers are speaking directly to all who are able to read this information.

Many have revealed they felt that these messages are being directed to them personally and that situations and teachings given often reflect exactly what they are going through at the time. Many readers of this material have felt this information is relevant to what they are dealing with now and feel extremely grateful for the confirmation and guidance being shared. I hope you too will find these messages and teachings pertinent and relevant to what you are experiencing in this lifetime as you walk your chosen path.

Wilma Jean Jones

"Emptiness is part of fulfillment. Let your "resources" fill the void left so that distinction of your purpose can be found. Expression is always self-explanatory. Therefore look inside and anchor all your beliefs "beside those still waters" that will take away your troubled view and renew your strength to recapture that which was lost but is now found to be adequate to pursue the course set before you, and as you reconcile your being to represent those qualities that have been left intact – God will see to it that although circumstances have been trying to say the least, your weariness will disappear as clouds once removed allow the sun to shine to dispel the gloom and darkness that has pervaded your countenance, and as once described before, a token of this presence will be 'deposited' to your account and books recorded in His name."

(Possible confirmation to record messages given in a book.)
I had been praying about it.

Message received by Wilma Jean Jones from Spirit
January 10, 1998

Foreword

Many readers of this material have a church based/bible based background. I was brought up attending a Pentecostal church. My uncle, a fiery Pentecostal preacher by the name of John W. Sullivan, founded the Full Gospel Tabernacle in Middletown, Ohio. I remember at a young age attending church and was amazed at the large crowds that would come to hear uncle J.W. preach his sermons. Readers with a church based/bible based background have learned and read about angels, guardian angels, and Archangels throughout their life. Readers who are more spiritual in nature or who have read metaphysical material have learned and read about spirit guides, spirit teachers, Master Teachers. Spirit teachers and angels are the exact same beings just viewed from a different perspective. They are all God's direct representatives.

Whenever you have a desire to contact your own spirit teachers/angels remember always to say a prayer asking for protection. As you relax your mind and drop down in level to receive visualize a white light of protection surrounding your being. This is the Christ light and offers protection from any negative influences that may be floating around looking for a warm place to call home. Then with assurance and confidence in this divine light of protection you are now open to receive whatever information your spirit teachers/angles desire to share with you. You will never be given any information you are not ready to hear. These sprit teachers/angels have our best interests at heart and will always reveal what is intended to help and support us at the time is it given.

The depth and quality of the messages and teachings received from spirit teachers/angels dictated through Wilma Jean Jones is unlike anything I have ever read before. The first person nature of these messages and teachings received allow all those reading this material to feel that they too are being spoken to on a personal level. The references to situations, events, circumstances, and prophecy received in these personal messages for Wilma and Michael appear to be woven with a universal thread allowing many who have read these messages and teachings to feel this information is being given to help them as well deal with similar situations in their life. These dictated messages and teachings carry powerful and supportive teachings, admonishments, encouragement, and hope. Sermons could be given from many of the messages and teachings that have been received.

This body of material not only offers proof of the existence of a spiritual realm outside this physical plane, but presents communications in the form of messages and teachings dictated from spirit teachers/angels who inhabit this spiritual realm. The first person nature in which these spirit teachers/angels refer to themselves throughout this material draws the reader to the inescapable presence that the spirit teachers presenting these messages have made contact through Wilma Jean Jones for a purpose. "We come when called. We are aware of your beings." These expressions are spoken frequently within these messages and these spirit teachers/angels express repeatedly their joy in finding such willing and receptive vessels such as Wilma and Michael to work with.

It is Wilma and Michael's hope these messages and teachings will inspire all readers of this material to be open to their own spirit teachers/angels in a manner that facilitates the support and love these teachers offer with unwavering loyalty to our cause. There is never a time when they are not present in all that we encounter in our daily lives.

These spirit teachers ask for nothing more in return than our recognition of their existence and our openness to their advice, guidance, and direction as their expressed goal and mission is to serve our Heavenly Father by serving us. Who among us in these times in which we live with all that we must deal with are not willing to be receptive to the help and guidance offered with grace and love from God's direct representatives?

Michael McAdams

Michael's note

The messages and teachings dictated directly from spirit teachers/ angels from the other side received through Wilma Jean Jones were recorded and single spaced typed exactly as given. The spirit teachers presenting this information have many times related their teachings in long sentences and with few or even no paragraphs throughout the entire message.

For the ease of reading and understanding these deep and thought provoking messages and teachings, I have on occasion divided extremely long sentences and passages into paragraphs so that readers of this material will not be overwhelmed by the depth and content of these teachings. Many times I have read certain passages two and three times just to make sure I understand the meaning these spirit teachers are attempting to convey.

These spirit teachers/angels speak with an authority and a perspective that instills a sense of awe that direct communication with spirit teachers from the other side is truly being recorded. Allow the messages and teachings presented in these volumes of An Angel Told Me So to inspire all readers of this material to make contact with their own spirit teachers/ angels. Their joy is in our recognition of their existence. They are here for the help, support, and guidance they offer with unconditional love as we make our way upon this journey we call life.

As you read this material ask for understanding and the manner in which these messages and teachings are pertinent to what you are dealing with in this existence. Allow the reception of these messages and teachings received through Wilma Jean Jones to be an inspiration so that you may also be receptive to your own spirit teachers/angels as you walk your chosen path.

Michael McAdams

Whisper in the hearts of man
The words of God

Wilma Jean Jones had received information before that had been dictated to her mind. Sometimes a message would come unexpectedly and she would reach for whatever was close by to take down what was given. But on this Saturday, August 13, 1977 Wilma Jean Jones felt led to sit down at the table in her kitchen where she had set up her typewriter to receive. Her kitchen was clean and spotless as usual and this was to be the location for receiving the messages and teachings that spirit teachers/angels had decided to share with her. She relaxed her mind and said a prayer asking for protection as she opened her mind to receive. She had lit a candle and treated this experience with great reverence as she felt privileged to be given this opportunity to communicate with these spirit teachers. At first the words came slowly. As she relaxed her mind three or four words would appear. Not hanging out in space but within her mind. Once she typed these words they would fade away and three or four more would appear. Paragraphs and punctuation were given as she took down these dictated words. This is the process in which these messages and teachings were received.

In this session which lasted about two hours she first received a message for herself and then received a message for her son Michael. Wilma made every effort to take down the words exactly as given and made it a point not to attempt to anticipate where the sentence was going but just went with what was being given. The messages presented in this session were encouraging in nature and complimented the effort put forth by both Wilma and Michael as they dealt with what life's journey was presenting them at this time.

The message given for Wilma promised that these spirit teachers/angels would be with her and guide her in all she would accomplish. Her attitude of love and service would carry her through that which she would deal with and they promised to be at her side throughout all her endeavors. This message for Wilma and the message for Michael were both offered from a first person perspective. "Time has proven your devotion to us". "We acknowledge your love". These spirit teachers/angels speak to Wilma in first person as they are truly present with her in spirit. The depth and quality of these teachings received and the personal nature of this material engages and allows readers to feel they too are being spoken to on a level that reflects what they personally are experiencing and speaks to the heart of those willing to accept the divine nature of these dictated messages. These messages reverberate with a universal thread that speaks directly to all sincere seekers of truth on a personal level as each reader feels they are being addressed as they deal with what is transpiring in their lives. These spirit teachers/angels repeatedly refer to themselves in first person as "we", "our", and "us."

Wilma's message is one of encouragement and comfort for that which she has endured in recent years and for that which is to come. "We watch over you. This is promised to you". Michael's message is one not only of encouragement but of greatness and gratitude for what these spirit teachers felt would be accomplished. Wilma was pleasantly surprised that the message given for Michael was signed with the name of the spirit teacher who was presenting this message. This was the first of many messages and teachings given for both Wilma and Michael where a name would be given for the spirit teacher or teachers who were presenting a message.

August 13, 1977

Wilma,

Trouble will come but you will not have to worry that anything will hinder what you are trying to do. Continue on your way and know that many are with you. (That is because you are just waiting for a message. This will be done.) What you desire you will accomplish. Nothing is impossible for you as your willingness to try has been acknowledged. Your courage has been shown. Blessings are bestowed upon you as you are patiently working toward a goal. Time will prove your devotion is true to us. Never think that all is in vain.

More will be given to you as you proceed with your studies. Know that always there has been a guiding hand upon you. When you are tested the hardest, you win the most. Sometimes the way is hard to walk but there is always a smooth road ahead. This must be your refuge. No one is trusted with such unless they are willing to walk ahead no matter what they see. In their way they will conquer all when they forge ahead with knowledge that they are supported in what they do. In knowledge that they are right; in knowledge that truth prevails and therefore no one has victory over you as you are protected.

You are blessed to us and we acknowledge your love, your interest, your desire to be close to us in all ways. Never fear. We will watch over you. This is promised to you. Come now. See the way is clear for you. Step forward and know there will be waiting for you a place of comfort, a place where you may rest from it all.

August 13, 1977

Michael,

We see that you are very important to your cause. Your mother can be of help in that she can relate to you things that may be hard for you to acknowledge yourself. You must be confident, be strong in your feelings when it is necessary that you make decisions in your interest.

Your attitude toward life has been tried and tested and you have proven the ability to see far beyond the horizon to heights unknown but by a few. This ability to see beyond the realities of this present life has enabled you to be empowered with gifts that ordinary people can never behold. This in itself is a gift. To be able to have insight into spirit world and to know their presence is with you; to know and conceive the very fact that existence one with the spirit is possible. No one person need feel that this is not acceptable. We are aware of you.

We feel your heartaches. We feel your restlessness. We feel when you are near to us. At times like these our hearts are gladdened by the closeness of your thoughts. Therefore as we are pulled in your direction, we come willingly. Happiness is ours and we give you a portion of that happiness to have as your own as you uplift us in spirit by your uplifting of spirit.

Many times we have chosen to be by your side. Many times we have watched over you. You knew that we were there but we could not let you know the reality of our presence. Now we are pleased that at last we can talk with you. That we can communicate this way. We are pleased with the progress you have made.

The power of commitment to you will be one of service. When we are called upon to serve you, you will feel our presence and know that we are there. Whatever you do is blessed. Whatever you attempt is supported by us. Keep yourself in such a manner that we might work with you more abundantly. This is not a demand. We do not mean that you must give up anything that you desire to do but only that you keep yourself open to us.

Circumstances may cause you some grief. This is temporary. Release will come. Know and have confidence in these messages. They are important to you and will be of help to you.

I know.
Your guide
Go now. I will be with you.

The following Thursday, August 18, 1977 Wilma again felt led to receive a message from spirit teachers. She was excited and hungry for what she believed was such a privilege to receive and was willing to dedicate the time and effort required to sit for such long periods of time to take down the words that were being given. She had been bothered with problems with her back for a number of years but was ready to endure the pain if that would allow these messages and teachings to continue to be received. Wilma was again prepared with her typewriter set up at her table. She lit a candle and said a prayer asking for protection. She inserted a blank sheet of paper into her typewriter, dropped down five lines and indented five spaces just as you would do to type a letter. As she relaxed her mind the words again began to appear.

The first message received was for Wilma and immediately spoke of the problems that must be dealt with in this physical world. Encouragement and the promised support from God was the main theme in this message. A name was given for the presenter of this message that suggested there were multiple teachers involved in this rendering.

The message received for Michael conveyed not only encouragement but included information about what he was destined to accomplish in this existence. The first person reference these spirit teachers' make to their presence and the closeness these spirit teachers/angels expressed for Michael advising him they will be at his side and available to his call brought the promises of love and support from these spirit teachers that much closer to his heart. The name given for the teachers presenting this message for Michael suggested again there were multiple entities involved in the presentation of this information.

August 18, 1977

Wilma,

Sometimes the way is very hard to comprehend the meaning of inner peace when problems in the physical world are hard to bear. However, have confidence in the fact that help and assistance is guaranteed you if you will but believe that this is given to you by a higher power. One that is so very high that you cannot conceive the fullness of it all. This world is not the end of creation. There is more than the imagination can comprehend. The universe is small compared to the Kingdom of God. Many years, which is your measure of time, have elapsed and yet man has not fully come to understand the fullness of God. His love and knowledge has never been fully received by man because he has chosen to turn a deaf ear toward the things that God has tried to show him. Many times people have been shown the way. Many times people have been told what to do but they have turned a deaf ear to the voice of God. When man comes to the realization that he must listen to the voice of God then he will know the true direction that he must take.

Many people are chosen but they do not heed the call. What sorrow is felt when we see needless suffering and heartaches do to the fact that people are unable to heed the voice that shows them the way out of their difficulties. Sorrow should not be a part of your life. God did not intend for this to be so. But in balance with the principle of God's love and without cooperation with the will of God, man will continue to go astray. Blessings await the man who becomes attentive to the will of God. Be not discouraged when life holds disappointments for you. Know that God is aware of your circumstances. He will not let you be alone.

Keep courage and faith and believe that God can deliver you from every adversary in this life. No one has victory over you. You must conquer because you have the strength, the faith, and the ability to believe in God and all His power and to know that to conquer is to be one with Christ. This must be your refuge. Be one with Christ. He will protect you and He will see that you have victory over all.

Your Guides

August 18, 1977

Michael,

You are sweet and your ability to show compassion at the time when it is needed is a credit to you. You will see a change in the people that you come into contact with. Your influence bears much weight. You have the ability to show other people the way when their eyes are blinded to the truth and life has led them astray. They are fortunate that they have been able to make contact with one such as you. Your ability to make yourself clear; your ability to get across a point that most people could not comprehend had they read the written word. Oh what a special gift you have.

You have been chosen to lead many on a righteous path that they would not have found their way if not for you. You see there are many who cannot accept what they have been taught. What has been revealed to you has been done so with a purpose. When you feel led to talk to someone know that this is a guiding of the spirit. Words will be given you to say to that particular person. You have done very well indeed. You have given food for thought to these who are hardened to the word and who find it hard to accept the truth as you have presented it. But rest assured that you have made your point clear.

You have done what was expected of you. You have done your job well. We are very proud of your progress and the fact that humility has become a large part of your being. This will enable you to now receive many of the gifts that you have longed for. Now you have opened a door. Your desire to truly help a soul in need has been recognized. This is truly a great show of humility. Love has been made a part of your life and now the fruits of your labor will bring forth many results that until now you did not know were possible.

Keep believing in the way that you have chosen to follow. You will not be disappointed. There are many rewards awaiting those who have the ability to follow their instincts and to know that there is a better life in store for those who will continue regardless of hindrances that may come their way. This is given to you. Doubt not. There will be many things unfolded that you will behold and understand the full meaning of such. This has been promised you many times before. We understand your circumstances therefore we will work with you diligently. We give you our pledge that we will be ever present at your time of need and desire. Know that we go with you. Know that we stand by your side. Know that ever when you call upon us we will be at your service. We are but few of the many who have been called to serve you. Many stand ready to help you when you need their services. Know that this is true. We watch over you constantly. We are ever aware of you. You are precious to us and therefore we await your call.

Your Spirit Guides

On Sunday, August 28, 1977 Wilma was again led to receive. She started really looking forward to these sessions even though they took quite a bit out of her. Wilma felt such a privilege to be able to receive these messages from spirit teachers/angels. These messages were being dictated word for word and this was a slow and methodical process. Wilma had been married for fourteen years and some of those years had been difficult. She had decided in her mind that she could not continue in a relationship with someone who did not seem to love or care about her any more. Wilma had not confided in anyone about her decision and was still working this out within herself. Her spirit teachers knew what she was going through, however, and they advised her and comforted her in this message. This was also another message where multiple entities seem to be involved in presenting this information. "There are many things that we have planned for you to do". "Because you look to us for guidance we will always be near to you". The plural first person references these spirit teachers make to themselves allows Wilma to be aware that multiple teachers are indeed presenting this information. August 28th was Wilma's birthday and these spirit teachers/angels presenting this message make note and offer her special greetings on this day of her birth.

Wilma also received a message for Michael in this session. Michael's message was one of continued encouragement and support for what was to come and the role that he would play in this existence. He was advised that "There are many teachers who will work with you…" and was told of guidance that was to come. The message for Michael was signed "Your spiritual teachers". This was the first time the name "Your spiritual teachers" had been given and once again it appears there are multiple entities involved in presenting this message.

August 28, 1977

Wilma,

There is a time when all good things must come to an end. When you believe in what is right and know that justice follows your actions, then you will realize that all that has been done in the past was for a reason and you are not to continue along a path that leads you to emptiness. When you come to know the fullness of God's great love you will be able to encompass many experiences that will bring to you the rewards that you deserve. This promise is not given to you to be taken lightly. When good is given then good should be expected by you. This is not the way that most people live their lives. Many people are concerned with receiving but do not realize that by giving of themselves truly without expecting a return that more will be given them. Comprehend what you are receiving today and interpret its meaning to allow you the freedom you so desire without any demands or strings attached as you are doing your best in the best way that you know how. You are not giving to receive anything. This is not your motive or intention and therefore what you allow yourself to experience is truly yours to have for the moment and to enjoy without feelings of any regret. While you are giving in this manner more is being prepared for you.

You are useful to many people and the way in which you go about helping others is appreciated. There are many things that we have planned for you to do. At some time you will be given the ability to see into the lives of others in a manner that will be significant to them and will enable them to find the right perspective in their own lives. Only those persons who come to you will you be concerned with. They will be sent to you in some manner or other and you will be able to distinguish between those who will accept you and your message of enlightenment and those who will refuse to believe and accept what is given as truth. Between these groups of people you will find a deeper experience which you will be able to translate as teachings from a higher entity who is now aware of your ability and desire to communicate in this way to bring help and encouragement to those souls who will realize and accept this way for what it is. When people tend to lean upon you know that by lending a helping hand you further that souls progress along the path. Acknowledge your ability to influence people to your way of thinking. Therefore you can be of much help to them because you are receiving instruction and guidance from higher teachers who will instruct you in the manner that you are to speak to these souls and will give you the thoughts and words that you are to say. Nothing will be given to a person who is not receptive in thought. Concern yourself with those who are open to you as you can be more effective with them. Because you look to us for guidance we will always be near to you.

Close the door to the past. Upon this door write the words, "I have surrendered all to God with love". When you finally do surrender all to God and know that your steps are now ordered and directed for your own best interests, you will not regret the sacrifice because in store for you are glorious experiences and fulfilling relationships and marvelous adventures that will take you to heights unbelievable in your present state of mind. Release from pressures will enable you to be in a position to accomplish greater things. Remember nothing is taken away but what that place is filled with more than what was thought possible.

We give to you from the storehouse of God many treasures. Bliss follows the man who can walk in the footsteps of God. Whatever you need to enable you to stand will be given to you. Search your heart to find your true self. When you come to the realization that you are truly God's child know that with this knowledge also comes all the responsibilities of being one with Him and also sharing a part of all He is. This means that you are to experience His love and protection and divine guidance in your life. Concentrate on this point that God shares His kingdom with those who acknowledge Him believing that He will grant to them all that He has promised. You are like a flower that has begun to blossom and lift its face toward its creator. Given the light from God's goodness you too will bring forth in all your glory all that you have been given to express in this lifetime. As the flower so reaches full bloom so will you. This will be accomplished by the faith that you are showing by accepting what is being given to you now.

Always we have watched you in anticipation of the day that you would acknowledge our presence and reach out to us as a child reaches for its parents secure that there will be found comfort and security from life's problems. We welcome the opportunity to serve you in this way. Accomplishments have already been recorded and by way of speaking to you we have found an instrument that we value very much. We will not let you suffer as a result of what you are doing for us. Watch yourself and see the great changes that are taking place. This is our gift to you. When enough time has passed you will be able to look back and see where we have been at your side. We are grateful for you. Be careful that you do not allow any room for self doubt. It is not a part of you. You are a special person and there will continue to be outstanding circumstances that you will encounter and will bring you much joy and love. Keep our love close to your heart as we are always aware of you. Continue on your way now. We love you and send you special greetings this day.

Your Spiritual Guides

August 28, 1977

Michael,

Remembering your devotion and desire to work closely with those whom you wish to help gives you a special place within our realm. Never give a thought to what you feel you should do about certain matters as a solution is already prepared for you. Given time you will see that the actions of other people who have affected your life will soon no longer be a part of you. What path you choose to follow will be the one meant for you as you will receive direction and be pulled toward the place that you are to be. Circumstances are not always clear and easy to see when you are so involved in what you are doing. This is only natural in your physical world. What comes your way is sometimes given to you as a test to see if you really want to follow the path that you have chosen. But when you come down to the final analysis you always seem to make the right decision. This is because you are following your natural instincts which are really given to you by God and you do rely on your natural instincts. This enables you to be free of persuasion. You ought not to worry. You can not please everyone whom demand of your time and devotion to their cause as most people have a tendency to put their cause first. You follow because you feel a need however remember that your needs have already been met. You are but to realize this. Nothing has come to you except by you.

When you prepare to go to different places where you are needed know that guidance is given to you so that whatever you may say or do will be blessed. This is what is meant by preparing yourself. You prepare yourself by the knowledge that all is already given to you. What steps you take have already been outlined for you. This is the course that you are to follow so walk with confidence. There are many teachers who will work with you and who will reveal each gift at the proper time. Come to know that fellow citizens will envy the work that you do and try to present a problem for you but to no avail. Protection is promised and great effort is put forth to see that you are not hindered in any way.

Continue on in your own beautiful way. You have made many souls gladdened by your willingness to try to be of help to them. Keep this thought in mind that where ever you go and what ever you do is blessed by spirit and sanctioned by God.

Your Spiritual Teachers

Two days later on Tuesday, August 30, 1977 Wilma prepared to receive another message from spirit teachers/angels. She was becoming quite comfortable taking down these messages and was thrilled with this line of personal communication. She appreciated what was being given and felt these messages gave her valued insight into what she was going through at this time. As she sat down at her table in front of her typewriter she relaxed her mind and waited to receive. Normally the message that would come through first would be for her but for some reason she did not "feel" the mental connection she normally would feel just as the words would start to appear. She tried for a number of minutes but nothing was coming through. She got up from the table and walked outside. It was a comfortable evening this late in August and as she looked up at the sky she said a prayer and asked if she really was supposed to receive a message at this time. The answer came back to her: affirmative. She went back into her kitchen and once again sat down in front of her typewriter. As she relaxed her mind the words began to appear only this time the message was for her son Michael.

Encouragement and comfort are the main theme of this message for Michael but with a continued reference to work that was planned for him to do. These spirit teachers advised that they had entered in a different manner this time. Possibly that is why Wilma had a more difficult time receiving than usual. These spirit teachers continue to make first person references to themselves. "Together we will see much accomplished". "Our desire is only to work with you in the spiritual light…" These first person references permitted Wilma to feel the closeness of these spirit teachers/angels as these messages were delivered and the spirit teachers themselves remarked about the pleasure they felt in sharing these moments with her. This message was signed "Your Spirit Teachers" and indicated again there were multiple entities involved in the presentation of this material.

August 30, 1977

Michael,

Again we meet with you. We enter this time in a different manner. Acknowledge your teachers. We meet to advise you tonight. Never give anything of yourself that you do not freely wish to express. Clever persons will try to manipulate you. You must not let this happen as it could impair your advancement along the path that you have chosen to walk. Most areas of your life are well under control. You allow yourself little room for pleasures of this world. We allow you more than you are accepting and feel that you can do and still perform the duties to which you have been called. Do not limit yourself. Many great works will be done as a result of the effort that you are putting forth at this time.

Keep yourself open to guidance that will come to you through thought waves being sent your way. We work only with those who are willing to believe and accept this way as being true and right. Nothing is lost by giving insight to your physical being but there is much to be gained by giving yourself the opportunity to work with us in the greatness of this task that must be done. Overcome obstacles that are keeping you from fulfilling your purpose in life otherwise you will find that disappointments lie ahead because you were meant for a higher purpose and only when you are free to fulfill that purpose will you enjoy the fruits of your labor and you were meant to enjoy the fruits of your labor.

Whatever is given to you, you must realize was given to you because you deserve it. Therefore, take delight in what is given to you to enjoy as you are to reap rewards along with the work that you do selflessly. When one soul gives to another without thinking of themselves and what they might gain for the giving, then are they given the greatest reward of all. You have done this many times now.

Oh, how great will be your rewards. Little things mean much at a time when needed and when received can mean much more.

Keep in mind that again many work with you. Together we will see much accomplished. Continue to walk as you are because the way before you is bright. Whenever your needs are many you must remember to come to us as we are here to supply your needs. Asking is a show of faith. We would be happy to serve you in all ways that we can. Again we stress the need for you to enjoy your life on Earth as it was given to you and all the greatness and goodness that God has given is to be yours. While you walk the path know that you may partake of life and its goodness because you are a part of it. We appreciate your willingness to abstain many things that you feel may hinder your progress with us. However, we are not demanding. We are not wanting to control your very being. Our desire is only to work with you in the spiritual light and therefore this is our only concern and interest. Be assured we walk with you. We come when invited. We love being near you. It gives us pleasure to share these moments with you. We go but we will return another time.

Your Spirit Teachers

On Thursday, September 1, 1977 Wilma was again led to receive. There were to be two messages that would come through in this session. The first message was again for Wilma and these spirit teachers/angels acknowledged that she had not received a message in the last session and chose to give her an explanation. Wilma's decision within her own mind that she could no longer stay in a marriage that offered nothing in the form of love and comfort weighed heavily upon her and she had told no one of her intentions. Still these spirit teachers offered her comfort and support and let her know that she would not be going through this alone. This message was of great comfort to Wilma as she knew not what the future would hold or how she would be able to sustain her home and have an income. These spirit teachers reassured her and let her know she had been chosen to do this work.

In this same session Wilma also received a message for her son Michael. His message advised that he would also be important in this work and that these spiritual teachers/angels "choose their vessels wisely". There was an interesting statement made by these spirit teachers regarding the manner in which this information was coming through. "We relate to you as it comes to us and is given to us for you to receive". This is interesting as it appears these spirit teachers are receiving information from yet a higher source as they reference being given information "from a variety of teachers"

The depth and quality of these teachings received and the personal nature of this material engages and allows readers to feel they are being spoken to on a level that reflects what they personally are experiencing and speaks to the heart of those willing to accept the divine nature of these dictated messages. The teachings in these messages given continue to reverberate with a universal thread that speaks directly to all sincere seekers of truth on a personal level as each reader feels they are being addressed as they deal with what is transpiring in their lives. Note the references by these spirit teachers' to themselves as "we" and "us." Both messages received for Wilma and for Michael were signed "Your Spirit Guides".

September 1, 1977

Wilma,

There is a reason why you are not receiving a message. There is a great importance being put on your time and you are being pressured by outside influences that are hampering your ability to freely concentrate on what we have for you. Keep this in mind that you are ever in our care and we will not stop waiting for your call when we are needed. We are aware of your difficulties at this time and we want to remind you that everything is being taken care of and you will not have to depend upon other people for your source of support. We want you to be happy and contented as you have tried to be to other people what you, yourself, would want to come to you. Possible circumstances are waiting for you as you have come to the place where much that has been reserved for you will now be brought to the surface. Time holds much in the way of problems for you. There is much you are needed to accomplish and yet there is still much work to be done. Organize your business and see if you do not feel better about yourself and then each thing will fall in place. We are aware and concerned for you but you are being taken care of regardless whether you feel things are going right or not. Rearrange your schedule to meet the demands that are necessary for you to attend to at this time. Pressure will be eased. You are very valuable to us and we need to see that things are well with you.

There will be many important decisions for you to make in the near future. Things will not be what they seem. You will have to use caution in dealing with other people and know that your needs will be taken care of and wisdom will be given you to handle the decisions that you will have to make. Long ago there was given to you a gift to hear these words and you acknowledged our call. This will not be taken from you as you are willing to participate and

23

you anticipate greater works and these will be given to you. Let us make a point clear. You are not to worry or fret about your physical world. We want you to be content and satisfied and it grieves us to see you upset needlessly. There are many things in your favor and one of these is the fact that you are loving and show true affection and therefore that is why we are also drawn to you. Want the things that please you as you are entitled to them. Those difficulties that you now face were brought on not by your failure to respond but because there is a force that is working in your life at this present time that is difficult to explain to you, however, know that where we are needed to stand by your side we will be there in great numbers.

Let us continue to be of service as we take delight in coming to you in this manner. Whatever is given is never taken away. It is only denied if you so choose it to be. There is so much more for you. We wait to give you all the rest as we are aware that difficulties are interfering at this time. Possible circumstances were mentioned before. We give you a definition. You may turn around and go backwards to what you were before or you may choose to move at a rapid pace to heights reserved for you and be given at that time all the gifts and rewards that will follow. If you so choose to accept, then we do not doubt but what you will choose the latter. We have confidence in your ability and we want to give you all that you desire to have. There is nothing that will not be given unto you if you will only believe that within yourself lie all the qualities that are needed to fulfill these experiences that you are seeking.

Come now to the place that we have made ready for you. It takes a little time to accustom yourself to these feelings that you are now experiencing but it will all come through. Never are you to feel that you are going to regret any action that you feel is necessary to take. What happens in the future will follow a plan that is designed for your success. There will be changes that will be necessary but acknowledge them as stepping stones to achievement. Follow your intuition and know that One is leading you to the place that you should be. This is the reason you have been chosen because you will follow your intuition and therefore we can easily work with you. Take your rest now and we will be with you again soon.

Loving you.
Your spirit Guides

September 1, 1977

Michael,

Take the instructions that have been given you in the past and know that again much power and energy is sent your way. There will be a difficult period in which you might feel that you are being neglected but this will not be so. Arrangements are being made to give you what you have been asking for to receive. Whether you receive audibly or through thought process you will receive it. You are centered now to receive the ability to communicate also. There are given to special people this gift. Those who do acknowledge us who will listen and heed our advice and instruction as you both are doing very, very well indeed. This is so appreciated. Willing instruments are not easily found. We choose our vessels wisely. We do not work without knowing that our accomplishments are assured and we know that as we work with you, you grow stronger, you try harder and this pleases us. This is why we intend to see that you are given much more than you have already enjoyed. Whatever seems to come your way now is a result of all the effort that you have applied.

There are still souls out there wandering and searching and thirsting for knowledge that you can supply. Rest assured you will be given a chance to experience the opportunity that lies ahead in this field of relating to other people the truth as you have come to know it. There are many who will listen to you and absorb what you are revealing to them for the first time. There will always be that One who will be with you regardless of the circumstances. There is a guiding light that goes ahead to lighten your path where ever you may walk. We will let you experience different sensations that will enable you to understand what other people may be feeling at certain times and therefore you will be able to understand what they are relating to you. Take this message and know that more will be given to you to direct you in the way that you have chosen to walk.

There is the possibility of receiving many, many important and decisive messages that can enable you to acquire knowledge that would not have come to you from any other source. We relate to you as it comes to us and is given to us for you to receive. This is an established way in which we work with those we have chosen to help along life's way. We are given much information from a variety of teachers. We enable them to work with you in this manner. There will be more given to you another time. We go but we return.

Spirit Guides

Nine days later on Monday, September 12, 1977 Wilma was again led to receive. She was surprised how often the messages were being given but remembered that these spirit teachers/angels had complimented her on her willingness to receive and that they would accommodate her knowing how hungry she was to participate in this work and how honored she felt to be a part of these sessions. These teachers speak of the many instructors who would be working with her and that even though difficult times lie ahead they would not be of long duration. For the first time since these sessions had begun an actual signature was given for the teacher presenting this information rather than a printed name. Wilma "saw" the initials L Z written in script and duplicated them to the best of her ability.

The message received for Michael in this session was again one of encouragement and comfort. They complimented him once again for being receptive to these words and spoke of the coming work that he was to do and the service to be performed. Ten specific points were given regarding the work that was to be accomplished and Michael was reassured that he would not be alone in this effort. These spirit teachers/angels promised to be at his side with help and support. This message given for Michael was also signed with initials written in script and appeared to be given by the same spiritual teacher who had presented Wilma's message.

Something interesting occurred in this message for Michael. For the first time these spirit teachers offered ten separate points for consideration and numbered them accordingly. These points were given and were double spaced between each one. Wilma was always careful to take down the words exactly as she saw them.

Note again as these spirit teachers/angels continue to refer to themselves in first person. "We" and "us" are used frequently as they present these messages. The teachings in these messages given continue to be woven with a universal thread that speaks directly to all sincere seekers on a personal level as each reader feels they are being addressed as they deal with what is transpiring in their lives.

September 12, 1977

Wilma,

While you wait there are many instructors who are preparing guidelines that you are to follow at this time. Some of the things that you are to do will be prepared for you in a manner that you can accept when it is presented to you. When it is time for you to move ahead in your progress things will become clear to you and you will understand exactly in what manner you are to proceed. Difficult times lie ahead in some areas of your life but these will not be of long endurance. Just like a moment in time they will all be over and you will not have had to suffer or experience bad circumstances that would last for any length of time. There are certain conditions that you must pass through but we will help you so that these will not be hard for you to bear. It is just a matter of time put in until you will receive the fullness of all that has been promised you. There are but a few more circumstances that need be fulfilled until you can come to the place where you are seeking to be at this time.

We will see that all goes well for you and that you will be given all the strength and fortitude that is necessary for these changes that are taking place in your life. These changes are necessary for you as you have reached a point in your life whereby you are utilizing energy giving faculties that enable you to commit acts of miracle workings that will be a tremendous awakening to those who surround you in this work you do. That this should be a part of you requires changes within your person. We are at work now engaging our finest specialists to see that you are filled with the necessary equipment needed to perform these miracles. There are changes that are taking place that you are not aware of but they will not harm you nor will they hamper you in your every day routine of living. You are endowed with a power and an ability to perform works of healing to other people who will acknowledge that they received this healing as a result of your touch on them. Lift your hands at this moment to receive what we have for you now….. There now. The gift is yours. Use it to the good of those who render their lives to God and who look to him in anticipation of receiving his blessing and who are in need of his help.

Which way you choose to walk will always be blessed and ordained but that will be up to you as to the direction you may wish to go. However, always we walk with you. Now that we are committed to serve you we are anxious to see you fulfill your obligations to this purpose. There are always ways that you will come to know as the proper way in which to use your new found gift. Love plays an important part in your life. Your heart will go out to those whom you feel love for and you will express your love at the same time. You are doing them this service. Combine your abilities to work with those who are in need of you. Whether you are torn between this decision or that, you will always be guided to make the right choice. Know this.

There are but few people who can listen as you do and few people who can be worked with in this manner. When you receive these messages you are influencing other people because there can be no doubt but what these messages are indeed being transmitted to you from a much higher power than you can imagine or comprehend at this time. However, one day you will understand. Little by little we have led you along but now we see that you are ready to receive in great abundance what was given to you to be yours. We keep some in store but we now give you this much more as you have proven that you will use what you are given. This pleases us. We consider you to be higher than the usual human being as you have the ability to comprehend this difficult manner in which we choose to speak with you. You are acceptable in very high circles of entities who look upon you with favor and who are seeking to work with you in the near future. They have planned great experiences for you and are anxious to see how you will respond. They are not the least in doubt that you will come through and will complete their utmost confidence in you and have all the joy in knowing that you are there when they choose to speak with you. You are constantly aware of their existence in your thoughts and they acknowledge this. They are willing to work with vessels such as yours who are so receptive and anxious to please.

Come to us again and let us counsel you further. We stand always in waiting and look forward with great pleasure in greeting you each time we have this opportunity.

September 12, 1977

Michael,

We will now deliver the message that is intended for our precious Michael. Little is known about the relationship that is given to you and Michael but realize special entities gather around as you combine your efforts in this manner.

Michael speaks of not receiving much when in reality he is given more than the angels. Look upon him with great reverence and admiration as he will lead many people. He is now becoming the person that he was intended to portray while in this lifetime. Combine your efforts. They are needed together to persuade these groups who feel that this is not to be in existence any more. Whether people choose to accept what has been given is not of any great importance. They will one day see where they were in error. Since you have come to us to hear the word of God and what His intentions are in each of your lives we agree that you are to be blessed in a particular endeavor that will enable you to be of the greatest service yet. Combine your efforts. What does that imply? It means that you are to work together when the opportunities arise and that this can be accomplished without creating a difficult position for you both.

There are many items to be considered at this time.

Number 1 - You can fulfill many obligations at the same time you are doing this work.

Number 2 - You can be at several places at the same time for the same reason and there be able to carry out this work.

Number 3 - You can undertake this work together and yet be separate individuals in that you each have your own way to go and each must fulfill his individual obligations.

Number 4 - What will be given to you to use must be put into action to be effective. We do not worry but what this will be done. Therefore, when we can assist you we will as this will need special arrangements that can be taken care of by methods that we have in our control.

Number 5 - When this is given to you to do you must not fret but rest assured that all is taken care of according to schedule and arrangements will work in your favor to see that all goes smooth.

Number 6 - We can not always predict what the other person may relate to you but we can predict what will take place as a result of this conversation.

Number 7 - When lessons are given to you in this manner we are teaching you step by step to control the situations that may arise when you least expect them and we give you a solution before it needs to be used. This is difficult for you to understand now but we advise you in the way we feel is best under these circumstances.

Number 8 - Whenever we come to you in this manner it is because we care and want to give attention to every detail that we feel is necessary that you understand. We carry with us much instruction for you at this time. We know that it is necessary that we guide you and control situations for you that will enable you to move about doing your duty and at the same time enable you to perform these tasks which are set before you to do. We attempt to deliver our messages in a very clear manner. Therefore, we will proceed.

Number 9 - There are many things you must do. Things that will contribute to your progress but it will come to you and you will not have to seek it out or apply yourself in any great manner. Just remain open to us and we will continue to fill you with the power that will enable you to do these things.

Number 10 - It will come easy. Do not concern yourself with what you are to do yourself but only know that as it is given it is given in abundance, it is given at the proper time, it is given at the moment it is needed. It is always given.

These are messages to instruct you in the methods that you are to use as you go about this special work. How very pleased we are that you will work together as you are close in nature and close by the tie that binds you in love as well as in service.

Suppose you are given a small token of appreciation. You may accept. It is given out of a show of appreciation and not in the way of payment. It is due, it is just, it is acceptable. You may acknowledge this with your ability to understand what we mean. Now we must come to a close. We have given you the first in a series of instructions that you can look forward to receiving on a regular basis as you will need this instruction to guide you along a straight line whereby you may walk without difficulty or without doubt or fear but what you are doing the right thing at this moment. Gladly we teach such receptive, endearing, loved persons as yourselves. Consider yourselves as one when you are doing this work because in reality you are one with God.

On Saturday, September 17, 1977 Wilma was again led to receive. It had been just a little over one month since she started committing the time in regular sessions to receive these dictated communications from spirit teachers/angels. Wilma began to look forward more and more to the time spent in contact with these spirit teachers and this direct line of communication. The closeness Wilma felt when these spirit teachers moved in allowed her to realize that God was indeed working through her. The presence of these spirit teachers/angels and the dictated messages being received were being given for a purpose that Wilma felt should not to be treated lightly. The spirit teachers themselves repeatedly expressed their joy and gratitude for Wilma and Michael's willingness to receive and incorporate this material into their daily lives and for the important work that was to come. The message given this day began:

"Unlock the door to find behind it the many wonders that we have promised you. This can be done by simply opening your mind to accept all these wondrous gifts that we have given to you."

In this simple opening these spirit teachers have presented the key that will open the door and allow all readers of this material the ability to put themselves in a position to receive communication from their own respective spirit teachers/angels. The key is an open mind. Spirit teachers/angels care not by what name they are called. Their only desire is to serve our Heavenly Father by serving us. The joy these spirit teachers feel when they find receptive vessels to work with is wondrous to behold.

This message presented for Wilma offered continued encouragement as well as promises of more instruction and guidance to come. One of the main themes prevalent throughout this material is that we should all become one with God and strive to make His teachings and principles our own. Wilma prayed about her decision to finally end an unhappy marriage and these spirit teachers promised her solutions to problems she would encounter. These spirit teachers/angels repeatedly assure us that we do not deal with problems alone but that they are here always by our side with comfort, support, and protection. God did not promise that we would go through life problem free. He has promised that He will be at our side as we walk our chosen path and go through our problems with us. These spirit teachers stated that upon their next session they would present a list of accomplishments and guidelines for Wilma to help her set goals for what was to come. Wilma's message was yet another message signed "Your Spirit Guides".

In this same session Wilma received a message for her son Michael. Michael's message contained a series of instructions that detailed many aspects of what was to come in the work that was expected to be performed. Again as in the previous message for Michael a series of guidelines and instructions were given and again they were numbered and presented in a double spaced format. These spirit teachers advised that these instructions were meant for both Wilma and Michael.

As this message was being received for Michael something very unusual happened. Wilma expressed "a sensation of filling up within her; a feeling of the actual presence of true spirit." The spirit teachers commented on this. Their answer is compelling. Michael's message was also signed "Your Spiritual Guides".

September 17, 1977

Wilma,

Unlock the door to find behind it the many wonders that we have promised you. This can be done by simply opening your mind to accept all these wondrous gifts that we have given to you. Use these wisely and you will see results that have been proven to be actual miracles. Listen again as we continue to speak to you in this manner which has proven to be so successful. There are a few things that we feel that you must do yet to complete the cycle. When you become one with the Father you will be able to see more clearly the reason for all that has transpired. Becoming one with the Father only means that you will completely put your trust in Him and in the promise that He has made you in the past. When you are one with the Father you are truly in accord with all His teachings and His principles.

There are more instructions and guidelines being prepared for you again at this time. There are ideal situations ahead for you so you can rely on the promises that we have directed your steps and have brought forward a plan whereby you may now see the pieces falling together and you will come to know that God's divine plan always works. When you are in doubt as to the outcome of circumstances that surround you understand that you are experiencing a common dilemma of man because confusion can very easily become a part of your physical world.

Let it be revealed now that your time of confusion is finally coming to an end. You see things in a different light now. You are accepting reality at last as you have been shown a greater purpose in your life and now the seeds of discontent are many. Worry not. There are solutions to your problems and we will see that these are given to you. When you come to us again we will have prepared for you a long list of accomplishments that will be available to you whereby you may begin to set your goals. Develop a method of operation that will guarantee you the success that you are looking for at this time. There are opportunities waiting and we will see that doors are opened for you. We will go now as we have important information yet to be given to you.

Your Spirit Guides

September 17, 1977

Michael,

Watch as we prepare for you again the series of instructions that are to help you and to guide you over difficult times and in those moments when you question the validity of some information that is coming to you at this time from another source. There will be many people who will come to you asking for help and at the same time have other purposes in mind. Continue to seek guidance. It will be needed. Let there be surrounding you a shield of sorts that no one can penetrate whose purposes are not sincere and just. You are vulnerable. You have many good qualities that are sometimes abused by other people. You allow yourself to give and to give more than other people are willing to give to you. You are a precious soul. We enable you to gain much information that will allow you an insight in dealing with these people. You must protect yourself. Don't let them take advantage of you. You need to use caution. There are circumstances in the making now that you are aware of. You will understand the advice just given and will know where to apply it.

Now to continue with our guidelines for your life as you have chosen this direction to walk and therefore we honor your presence with us at this time. May we be of the utmost help to you. Always know that the instructions that are given in this series shall be shared by the two of you so that as you combine your efforts you will be more effective.

Number 1 - When the time comes for you to work together there will be a tremendous amount of energy being felt by the two of you.

Number 2 - While you go about your daily task there will be an ever abiding presence with you at all times.

Number 3 - You are both aware now that you are not truly involved in the material aspects of what you are doing.

Number 4 - When you present yourselves to those people with whom you will eventually come to meet, hold yourselves in high esteem because you are chosen by the Father.

Number 5 - Let there be renewed confidence in your abilities because indeed you have now been strengthened.

Number 6 - This happens as a result of your ability to be persistent and to pursue that which you have confidence in and in which you have placed your trust.

Note: At this point Wilma expressed a sensation of filling up within her; a feeling of the presence of true spirit. They commented:

Yes, we gather close to you. Take this item as a personal one. How we love to work with you both. How receptive. How open minded. What jewels you are. What love you express. Oh how blessed you are to us. What closeness we can experience with you. Let us continue.

Number 7 - There will be a certain person who will advise you in coming months as to the needs of those who will need your help and who can benefit from what you have to offer at this time.

Number 8 - There are many works for you to perform and you will be given ample time to see these all come about. You will be amazed at what you see but know that because you have put forth the effort you are experiencing the fruits of your labor.

Number 9 - Continue to remember those in prayer who are far away from you at this moment but nonetheless are as dear and as much in need of your healing touch as those with whom you can make actual contact with.

Let us clear up a matter that has been some cause for disconcertment. There have been times when you have been unable to fulfill obligations that you felt were necessary and therefore it was important that you meet these obligations. Know that your steps are guided. Your direction is clear. Whatever may come your way is done so for a purpose and a reason. It will always work out for the good of all concerned so know that whatever may come or go you are where you should be at that time. You are both very conscientious when it comes to fulfilling obligation. In the past sometimes this has been a problem for you but now the load is lifted. All will be done in accord with the plan outlined and given you to follow. It will not all be on your shoulders. Allow yourselves some peace of mind when it comes to knowing what you must do and what you can do and what is expected of you.

While you go about your daily routines you are being filled constantly with renewed energy which will enable you to perform these great miracles and works that are to now become a part of what you do. How great will be your strength. How great will all that has been given to you be multiplied in excess of what can be given. You will always have within you extra strength and energy to allow you to continue on when you know that by all rights you should be exhausted. This is how you will know that there lies within you a special radiation of power that is given you because you have asked for and in faith accepted. There will be a time for you when you will know and realize what benefits can be yours as a result of your willingness to be a part of this great work.

Go now and each time that we meet with you in this manner we leave you with renewed energy to allow you to accomplish more in the amount of time that you have to complete the daily work that is yours to do. No time is actually lost. You gain much because you are willing to devote this time from your day to communicate with us and we so appreciate this that we will allow you to make much more progress than you would have thought possible. God bless and keep you as you are worthy souls and we need to have communion with those who are indeed acknowledged by God.

Your Spiritual Guides

On Sunday, September 18, 1977 Wilma was again led to a session with spirit teachers/angels. It was late in the afternoon on this Sunday when she started this session and she did not finish the second message until later that evening. Wilma's devotion to this work was untiring as she was ever faithful to the call and her willingness to be a receptive vessel to the teachings that were being offered took precedence in her day to day activities. Wilma was never "too busy" to receive. She would not let these spirit teachers down.

Is this session Wilma received a personal message for her and a message for her son Michael. Wilma's message was again one of encouragement and these spirit teachers complimented Wilma on her ability to convey the spirit of God through the light that shone about her being. Wilma was advised her closeness to God and the Holy Spirit that surrounded her would affect all those she would encounter. Note again the personal reference these spirit teachers make to themselves as "we" in this message for Wilma. However, this message for Wilma was signed with the singular initials L.Z.

Michael's message spoke of those he would enlighten and show the way as his ability to receive and share teachings being given would draw many to his person. These teachers cautioned Michael regarding business decisions and advised to him to insure that effort was applied in the proper perspective to achieve the desired results so that time and energy would not be spent in unproductive activities.

Michael's message also contained personal references by these spirit teachers to themselves as "we" and "us". The spirit teacher who presented Wilma's message and signed it with the initials L.Z. also presented Michael's message; however, this spirit teacher's name was given in a different manner.

September 18, 1977

Wilma,

We welcome you. This finds us once again gathering together to furnish you with information that will prove to be helpful in the future. There are a number of items we wish to discuss with you. There are circumstances that are now unfolding that will permit you to go about your way in more freedom than you have experienced in the past. There is always a light ahead that you may look to because the light that shines is the spirit of God. There are wonderful and beautiful ways in which to describe the spirit of God. It can be expressed in these words of wisdom. Let your light so shine that others may see the Christ in you. What beauty can be found in truly being filled with the Holy Spirit and what wisdom can come from knowing that God is the all and overpowering force in the universe today and by this means many will come to know that God in His perfect wisdom is expressing through those individuals as yourselves the true meaning of His spirit and the manifestation of His works.

Wisdom is being given you as you yourself allow the light of God to shine forth from within you. His beauty will be part of your person. His love will control your every movement and the expression thereof will be done unto the Father as you go about doing good to others. His light shines brightly within you and radiates to encompass those who surround you in this work and those who are a part of you. Knowledge also is being given to you so that you may impart the words of God in a manner whereby they will carry much weight and power. Lo, the man who walks close to the Master walks in peace with himself and others. This is the way in which God intends you also to walk. There will be those who will criticize and those who will find fault and doubt that you are walking as close to the Master as you really are but pay them no mind. They are incapable of passing judgment.

That place of which we have spoken of before that we felt you should come to has now become a reality for you. What you do now will leave a great impression upon those who know you. We went before you and made the way clear so that you could see and know what is best for you to do. This is a time of great opportunity for you. Mother has been a word that has implied much to you and you have tried to fulfill all the obligations that lie therein. You have done well. Let there be peace within you. Note also that what you have always tried to do has always been in the best interests of those you love as well as for yourself. You have shared what has been yours to give. Note also the time for giving of yourself to those who have intentions of holding on to you for selfish reasons has been permitted up to now but the way is now clear for you to consider all the alternatives and to know that to settle for less than what you are entitled to would only be a useless waste of your time and energies. Your main purpose in life has been one of service and you have completed your duties as far as those obligations to those in need of more than you can take care of.

Consider this when you contemplate what is now to take place in your life. You are truly free and clear of any obligations you might feel are pressing you. This need not be a reason for your present difficulties. It is only to let you know that whatever lies ahead for you, you can accept knowing that you have done your best to fulfill your needs in areas that needed to be filled.

Come now and enter into a new phase of being and thinking and knowing. You are intended to be a great leader of many souls and your past is now a part of you that you can look upon with satisfaction that you did as well as you could under the circumstances. Little accomplishments add greatness to ones life. You have had many of

46

these. The time has come for you to now enjoy a portion of your life that is reserved for your pleasure. Consider this we ask again as you contemplate what lies ahead for you. You alone know what is best for you because you are now divinely guided and led and no longer will you walk without the assistance of One who loves you and cares for you as His very own.

L. Z.

September 18, 1977

Michael,

Time has come when you will discover that there are great expectations that have been acknowledged by us and are now being given to you. There are many such gifts bestowed upon you that will allow you to be the kind of person that you wish to be and you will now be able to reap the rewards that have been long past due. When you accept the circumstances that surround you now at this time you will be able to see and to know that once again in the face of adversity you allow yourself to rise above it all. This is an admirable trait that you have and when you are allowed to look back upon your life as you will one day you will understand all the little inconveniences and know that even such as these are used for a purpose. Then have you noticed when time has passed to a certain point. What has transpired is no longer important to you and in this way you are able to dismiss from your mind those things if collected and allowed to remain for frequent examination would only tend to make you depressed and troubled. But you have a way of showing your superior nature in that you can lift your thoughts to higher planes and know that your journey upon this Earth is but a span and all that takes place herein will be of no real significance in the end. Trouble free existence is rare indeed.

Thus we try to compensate you in other ways so that you may have a measure of joy as well. While we continue to help you we also continue to see that plans are made ahead that will help you to complete what you have in mind at this time. Sometimes we may impress you through thought forms as to the correct deduction that you must assume. This is why we caution you in previous messages. You are to now prepare yourself to gain entrance into a new perspective when it comes to the business part of your life.

Notice that we use the word perspective. That is for a purpose. You must consider each direction to see that the final outcome coincides with the amount of effort and time put into a particular project. Weigh the many advantages and disadvantages before you in advance. There will be more opportunities awaiting you in these areas and therefore it need not be necessary for you to commit yourself at this time.

Not every opportunity is necessarily a good one for you. As we said, look with the proper perspective. Use your abilities and your talents so that God may be exalted and by this we do not mean that you are to conform to any set pattern but you can have many diversified activities and still exalt God by the manner in which you conduct yourself. You are given a special ability to get your point across. This will lead you when you find it necessary. You will be able to see the way clearly and be able to make this understood to those who are to be involved in this project. Your understanding of what we are giving to you will be necessary for it to be effective for you. Your depth is great. Your vision is wide. Your heights extend unto the heavens. Great is the power being given to you and we use this manner to communicate with you because you have chosen to listen and to adhere to the advice that we freely give because you, yourself, freely give.

Consider all that we have spoken tonight. Let there be a peace within you also. We consider these moments to be very great accomplishments on the part of the two of you and when we are ready to commit ourselves to the service of those whom we serve we indeed commit ourselves fully and completely so that we may carefully guide you in the right way and in a manner that you can understand and come to know is our way.

We love you and intend to continue all the circumstances involved in your life at this time in order that we may best serve you to our fullest extent. Try to establish a complete and exact set of standards whereby you may follow our directions and know exactly what is to be done and in what manner. The procedure will be simple, the manner will be easy. The purpose always to serve God.

L. Zebelish

Five days later on Friday, September 23, 1977 Wilma was again led to receive. Wilma's message contained for the first time for her ten numbered declarations or instructions presented as guidelines that would fulfill promises made and reveal much that was to come. As promised a series of instructions and guidelines were offered and given with stated confidence that these instructions would be incorporated into the lives of both Wilma and Michael. These spirit teachers/angels had stated before that any instructions and teachings given should apply to both Wilma and Michael. There was a signature given to this message for Wilma but she was unable to make it out clear enough to duplicate.

In this same session the message Wilma received for Michael presented something unexpected. This message was unique and an occurrence happened to Wilma that had never happened before. As Wilma "saw" the words she was receiving for Michael the words appeared for the first time in a double spaced format rather than single spaced as in all previous messages. These teachings and instructions were given in short declarations with numerous references to the future and what was expected.

The beginning of this message given by spirit teachers/angels stated that Michael "was entitled to the choice between influence and persuasion and abilities to perceive truth." Michael's response made later after he had read this message was that his preference would be to have both and vowed he would use both gifts wisely.

Michael's message was signed with the initials of the same spirit teacher who had presented previous messages.

September 23, 1977

Wilma,

There is a governing force at work at this time. When you apply your energies your attraction creates a force and puts into motion the wheels that turn in the universe to see that the proper system is followed so that the information that you will receive is given in the proper perspective at the proper time and when you most need it. There are by-lines and guidelines that must be followed to the letter as there is form and order to the way in which we go about our business. When you are entitled to receive new information and instructions it will come to us and then we in turn promote the ideas to see that they come across to allow you to perceive their true meaning. When in service as you are you are expected to rely upon the information given you as it is necessary to your growth and promotion as far as service goes and as far as your progress is concerned. Need we go into deeper explanation for you to understand the workings of our world... We appreciate your understanding.

There are so many things to be discussed and so many avenues on which we could travel. There are endless explanations and important matters that you would find of interest because of your curious nature and your interest as far as our world goes. There will be a day when we will meet you and there will be a great reunion. This will be something to look forward to. Now to business. There are explanations due you. However, we choose at this time to continue with our line of instructions as you will be needed in the near future to perform the works that we have spoken of before and therefore you will need the information that we are now about to give you.

Number 1 - There are certain individuals waiting to see if you can deliver what has been promised you. Never fear. It will come and you only need to be present at the time.

Number 2 - When you reach forward to touch those whom you will be working with know that as you reach out at that particular moment your flow has already begun.

Number 3 - Watch for signs that will tell you in what direction you are to move and work accordingly.

Number 4 - There will always be a moment in which you will have an opportunity to give advice on how to influence oneself to correct thinking and positive mental attitudes that will allow that person to help themselves.

Number 5 - When you are given a message for a particular person there will be a divine working in that person's life as a result of what they receive from you.

Number 6 - There will be given great power to erase the illnesses and handicaps of those who come before you.

Number 7 - This is what was meant by the explanation given beforehand that you would receive all that is intended for you in a manner that you can understand and accept and will be easy for you to comprehend and put to use.

Number 8 - Many souls are waiting for you. Do not disappoint them. We have confidence that you will follow through as you have much compassion for those less fortunate than yourself and can consider their misfortune in terms of understanding and sympathy for their predicaments.

Number 9 - When you surrender yourself to the purpose for which you are intended you will see many great works and miracles performed because of your willingness to reach out to those in need. Always consider the alternatives. You are given these gifts but you are not commanded to use them. They are divine and mean much in your eyes and therefore you will take great pleasure in exercising your rightful position because you will experience the joy and relief that is felt by those with whom you work. Consider this when you choose your path. To take this step forward will mean you will receive great rewards by witnessing the results of your labors. Whisper in the hearts of man the words of God. Acknowledge His greatness and know that inner peace follows His leading.

Number 10 - This has been a very crude attempt to explain what we need you to do in order to exercise the power that has been given to you and to help you understand that along with this power that has been given you, you also carry a message that must be presented and explained to those souls who are either misinformed, misled, covered with darkness, sinking in the depths of depression and trouble and in need of spirit direction to lift them and allow them also to see the light of God's goodness and to find direction for their lives. You are meant for a dual purpose. Along with your healing abilities His message of enlightenment will be given to you that you might pass on to others that which is given you and therefore a teacher/leader will be your purpose also.

While you remain in this state of mind let us further reconcile you to the fact that there are entities at work at the present time preparing instructions for you that must come through proper channels to be effectively presented and therefore it has been with some hesitancy that we have presented this material in this manner tonight. We are aware of difficulties; however, we surmount every obstacle because we are in a position to do so. This will be a continuation of the series we spoke of before and we must get to the point and make it clear what we are trying to accomplish and therefore bear with us as we desperately try to communicate in a very exact and uncomplicated language. See what we have in store for you. This will be given to you later and perhaps the difficulties that have been present this time will be cleared.

Signature blurred

September 23, 1977

Michael,

Consider this. You are entitled to the choice between influence and persuasion and abilities to perceive truth. When you are given directions, know that by this very act there are those behind you who are consciously aware of your being and your purpose and your need of their correct instructions. We come to you bearing good tidings. There are difficult explanations. We will do our best to be understood. Complex situations present themselves. Divinities now appear. There will be great teachers and instructors. Now we heed the call. Calm follows the storm. Perplexities cease. Obvious circumstances control your being. Exact statements will be given. Tact must be incurred. Possible solutions now are in sight. Power is available. Initiative prevalent. Light revealed. Conscious awareness open to enable insight now being revealed. Stipulate your intentions. Consider all alternatives. Revelations will come. Forward progress will avail much. Teach. Reconcile your thoughts to enable you to use that which has been given to you tonight. You are able to now walk over the threshold that awaits you and enter into a dimension that will enable you to become great beings and great interpreters of divine endeavors with divine instructors and to travel with those who have walked beside you all along; to enter now into that place which holds many great wonders and revelations that will thrill your very being and enable you to liken yourself unto those who lead you.

While you remain in this state of mind let us remind you that complications are soon to be ended. Know that there lie ahead great experiences. This is just a beginning for you.

We acknowledge your interest and concern for those with whom you are working now. There will be a happening that will encourage you to know that knowledge that has been given you will now find an outlet whereby you may utilize that which has been given you and your ability to do this will summon to you those great teachers who stand ready to fill you with the necessary power when you are asked to deliver this message of which we speak.

Let there be a quiet calmness when you are asked interpretations and meanings as you will be given the proper explanation at that time. Preserve your knowledge. It will be of use to you one day. Let there be an affirmation within yourself that you are indeed called upon to perform feats that will require certain amounts of knowledge that you have been able to retain and conceive in that you have been able to see beyond what was written and able to comprehend its meaning where others might find it impossible to even comprehend its basic meaning. What you are given has much depth to it.

We regard you very highly. We trust you with much. Never fear. We walk ever so closely beside you, behind you, around you, and cover you with our protective blessing and shower you with the light of God's love and enable you to rise above the mundane experiences of this life and to know and to realize that there lies before you much in the way of great expressive relationships and meaningful experiences that will enable you to acknowledge that these were given to you in return for all the sacrifice that you felt were necessary and did so in the way of showing us your good intentions. Little do you realize how much we make note of. Go now. Rest and walk in contentment. We wait for your call.

L. Z

On Sunday, October 2, 1977 Wilma was again led to receive a message from spirit teachers/angels. These messages were being given and received more frequently now and the spirit teachers continued to express their joy and gratitude for Wilma's continued willingness to participate in this effort and for being so receptive to their communications on this high level. The promised closeness of these teachers and the continued emphasis on our relationship with God throughout our existence is the foundation upon which any and all communications with spirit teachers are based. These times of closeness and rapport with our spirit teachers assures us that spirit teacher/angel communications are real, desirable, and achievable for everyone with a sincere desire to participate with faith and confidence that these communications are given from God's direct representatives.

Is there one among us who would turn away and refuse such help, advice, assistance, and love in our hour of need? With the protection and divine guidance of our heavenly Father and His grace given to us upon which all things are accomplished we go forth in this existence striving always to keep an open mind and open heart with our intentions laid before us for our own spirit teachers/angels to see. Be not afraid of that which in this manner is given for our protection and guidance. Blessings are given to those who will allow these teachings to be borne upon their heart and fulfill the destiny of God's direct representatives who so graciously and lovingly work with us always in the name of the Father, the Son, and the Holy Spirit.

Wilma's message was a high teaching of encouragement and promised increase in her ability to receive and comprehend what was to be given. These spirit teachers continued references and promises of service for Wilma and Michael reflected the theme of many of the messages being received. Service to others as a deliberate choice is the key that enables these communications and empowers the gifts and abilities that are forthcoming for all who would receive. Wilma's hunger for deeper and more explicit material was acknowledged and was promised to be revealed. She was advised that her acceptance and willingness to receive was all that was required for the desired depth and quality of these teachings to come through. A signature was given by the spirit teacher dictating this message for Wilma, however, the signature was blurred and she was again unable to make it out.

Michael's message received in this session was most promising and unique as these spirit teachers/angels gave high praise and appreciation for his effort and accomplishments that had been brought forth and for Michael's effort to reach even higher in receiving and incorporating these teachings into his existence. At this point in the reception of this message Wilma was given a "vision" which she makes note of and describes in detail. Promises of future benefits and teachings were given and Michael was advised that great endeavors would be supported by these spirit teachers and that even greater opportunities would be made available.

This message was one of the most personal messages yet given by Michael's spirit teachers and their expression of love and devotion for his effort upon their behalf was moving and touched his heart. These spirit teachers greeted Michael as brothers in purpose and intent and promised a personal greeting when that prearranged day they would meet would come to pass. The signature on this message received for Michael was unique and no signature such as this from spirit teachers had ever before been received.

October 2, 1977

Wilma,

This message contains the information that is needed at this present time. There are many who need your advice and expression of love and your ever willingness to control this procedure has greatly increased your power and ability to receive that which is given to you in a manner that is difficult to conceive, however, your progress has been ever constant and you have increased the power at hand by constantly being aware of us and desirous of communication that will allow you to see into the realities of the universe and know truth that will not be revealed but to a very small handful of people. Allow yourself the opportunity to perceive what we have given you, therefore reflect upon it. Consider the alternatives.

Come to know your place in life and realize that the needs of others are to be important to you always. There comes a time when we must choose between those who hold for us the expectations that we have and those with whom we may find great rapport with. Little can we accomplish when we are torn between implications that cause us to remind ourselves that we are unworthy of what has been given to us when in reality we are given that which we have been promised as a result of deeds of kindness and thoughts of God and a desire to walk ever so close to Him and to know His favor and aware that He is supreme being and therefore all that we do must be with regard for Him and the fact that as His creation we are therefore united with Him in spirit and being and must always strive to be that for which He created us and allowed us to be that we may glorify Him and behold the brightness of His being.

In the stillness you will hear the voice of one who listens to the very heartbeat of your being/entity. When you least expect this presence know that always there is beside you one who bears the responsibility of your instruction and who guides your way in preparation for the day that you too will become a guiding force in the lives of others. Prepare yourself for a meeting in which you will recognize the one who leads you and who will continue on behalf of your progress into a greater internment at which time you will learn and understand great mysteries and revealments of consequent happenings that will allow you to see the workings of this mysterious force that controls more than you are aware of.

There are many sequences to what has been revealed to you thus far. There will be an advancement on your part to allow you to enter into an area that has thus far been forbidden to you but now that you have accepted and appreciated all that has come your way and are hungry and desirous of deeper and explicit happenings we want to share with you what we feel will benefit you in your work and will forward your progress at a rapid pace. This information will prepare your mind for what lies ahead for you. There will be no fear within your being as you are closely associated with us in thought and deed and therefore as we come to you we are to be one with the other. Acceptance is the whole. Endurance will mean more to you because you have experienced so many instances where you have had to endure but only for short periods.

Show yourself to be worthy only in the manner of your acceptance. We require no more effort than this. Your acceptance has been the greatest gift that you could give to us and we will see that you are given in return that which you so desire and choose to do. This much we promise as we are intended to fulfill your wishes at this present time.

Signature Blurred

October 2, 1977

Michael,

This happens to be an anniversary of a time when you came to us in response to our call. There was a man who met you and entered into your life by showing you that you were capable of performing miracles in your own right. This has been a year of enlightenment and growth in which you have proceeded with such speed and accuracy that you have excelled in every area that we presented to you and therefore we congratulate you and wish to express our great appreciation for all that you have accomplished and your continual interest and affirmation that you wish to go higher in your development and reach a pinnacle whereby you may be able to look out and see far, far into the future existence of this universe.

Note: Here Wilma described seeing a vision of Michael sitting upon a pinnacle observing a vast horizon with an unending universal sky overhead.

This has been a revelation of what is to come to you by way of your expression of the knowledge that you hold within your being. Much has been revealed to you that you are now coming to realize will be useful to you and avail much. There are studies that will be given to you to remind you of your purpose and will give you an outline whereby you may be guided in the work that you now do. Still continue to merge yourself together so that you may attain those heights for which you reach out for. There is awaiting you benefits that will enable you to continue in a manner that will prove that you can accomplish what you seek to accomplish and will be given all the necessary equipment that will be needed for you to proceed in this manner in which you have chosen to proceed. Whatever you seek to do will be supported by us as we know and are aware that you only seek these things so that you might have a greater opportunity and be in a position whereby you might be able to enlighten those with whom you come in contact with. Nevertheless, whenever there is a need for more support it will be given you.

There is a need that you now have want to be fulfilled. We see that you are entitled to what you desire and therefore we will see that you are fulfilled in the way you want to feel fulfillment. Come to us for every need that you have desires for and trust in our ability to do these things for you. This has been a special greeting in as much as we were thrilled at the moment you decided to become a part of our endeavor to help those souls of this universe to find contentment, healing for their sufferings, and a way of life that pleases the innermost being that is Christ-like and truly belongs to God himself. Whatever may take place from this day forward will always be a consolation to us that we were the very first to enlighten you and gain your confidence and therefore we will always feel a closeness in spirit with the one we have come to love and to know.

We greet you as brothers in purpose and intent and one day look forward to emerging to greet you when that day that has been so arranged comes to pass.

Loving you,
Spiritual Brothers

PHOTO GALLERY

This sweet relationship of mother and child is so special, and so rewarding, that it cannot easily be described in words. Yes indeed, the opportunity to guide this new life toward its destiny can only be seen as a precious gift from God.

A mother is an angel from God.

Wilma and Mother – 1942

Sherman Street, Dayton, Ohio. Wilma age 12. Mother Age 42

Mary Culbertson, Wilma Jean's mother, was a great influence on her life. Mary attended a Pentecostal church and was called to the ministry when she was 30 years old. Mary on many occasions was given, dictated to her mind, sermons and words to songs which she sang in church. Mary had been diagnosed with sugar diabetes and had taken insulin shots for a number of years. She had been taken to a hospital in Columbus, Ohio in September of 1950 as her condition had worsened. As she lay in her hospital bed and prayed she saw a vision of Jesus and words to a song began to be dictated to her mind. She picked up paper and pencil and wrote down the words. She would later say the words came as fast as she could write. Sound familiar? She later sang "this testimony" in many churches as an inspiration to others. Mary Jean Culberson was healed of sugar diabetes that day and for the rest of her life would never take another insulin shot.

Inspired from Mary's hospital experience. Written
in pencil, typed for preservation.

"As Jesus Stood There"
By Mary Jean Culbertson

Was early one morning on a September day
When in a hospital on a sick bed I lay
A patient of doctors and nurses was I
And a patient of Jesus and to him I did cry.

- 2 -

I told him my story through tears of despair
As I opened my eyes I saw him standing there
In a robe of pure white, so lovely and fair
Graced the scene of that moment as Jesus stood there.

Chorus

Was Jesus I saw, Oh praise his dear name
Was Jesus I saw, to him will I cling.
Tho life be like flowers that bloom every day
Tho some may be lovely, while some are not gay.

- 4 –

In love and great mercy, he stretched forth his hand
And while standing there he gave his command
I felt a sweet wave of peace over me roll,
Then joy and gladness enraptured my soul.

By faith I could sing and praise his dear name
My illness was gone, and I felt not the same
My pain and despair then drifted away
On the wings of the morning, on that September day.

A garden of flowers marked the scene of him there
While some were so lovely, there were some not so fair
But the presence of him, it so filled the air
And made life sweeter as Jesus stood there.

Wilma – Sunday best after church.

Wilma Jean had given her life to Christ at the age of 11.

Wilma Jean was an inspiration to all around her.

Wilma Jean passport photo

Wilma Jean was given the opportunity on three occasions to
visit the Holy Land. Her first trip was in September of 1979.
She had traveled with a church group from Cincinnati, Ohio.
It was a non stop ten day tour but she said it was amazing and
she was anxious to go back if she could. Wilma didn't know
at the time she would be able to return on two more trips.

Wilma Jean and a dove sent from God. She named it Spirit.

Wilma Jean had been lying in the sun in her back yard one day when a beautiful white dove flew down and landed close to her. Wilma had always cherished white doves and had one on her business card. She spoke softly to it and it walked up to her. The dove let her pick it up. She felt it may have been someone's pet dove that had flown away.
Wilma kept and cared for the dove and bought it a mate.
She named the mate Little Mama.

Spirit and little Mama

Wilma would keep these doves and two offspring for years.

Wilma's son Michael

Wilma's son Michael McAdams home on leave from basic training before being stationed in Germany for two years.

Wilma's son Michael

Wilma had asked for and received a special message for her
son Michael for his birthday. The typewriter Wilma used
to take down these messages and teachings can be seen on
the left. The message she received for Michael's birthday
is on top of the cake box. This table set up in her kitchen
was where she received the dictated messages and teachings
from spirit teachers/angels for twenty two years.

These Spirit Teachers/Angels found a willing
instrument in this beautiful soul.

When the student is ready
A teacher will appear

Ten days later on Wednesday, October 12, 1977 Wilma was again
led to receive. A new type of teaching was presented in this message
as these spirit teachers/angels chose to become quite specific in
their instructions as to the manner in which the concentration of
energy combined with visualization can be used and directed. The
technique contained in this message is available for everyone to
use if they so desire. "Ask and you shall receive. Seek and you shall
find. Knock and the door shall be opened unto you." Each of these
promises requires but one thing from any sincere seeker and that is
a positive action upon our part. Know that you have access to this
same line of spirit teacher/angel communication. All you have to do
is ask. By Wilma's acceptance and her desire to help others, these
teachings were being received. Wilma's open mind and willingness
to serve has allowed her to find this avenue of communication. By
Wilma's willingness to dedicate her time to these sessions she has
knocked and the door has been opened unto her. A signature of the
spirit teacher presenting this message for Wilma was given but this
signature was blurred.

Wilma also received a message for Michael in this same session. In Michael's message these spirit teachers/angels speak of the absolute and profound truths contained within these messages as they have been presented by divine guidance. They speak also of the presence of God within our beings and His devotion to our purpose as we walk our chosen path in this existence. This message speaks of the divine son Jesus and the manner in which He chose to present Himself to those who walked the Earth at that time. Jesus chose a form they could understand and relate to and be accepted as "one of their own".

A signature for the message presented for Michael was given but it too was blurred.

October 12, 1977

Wilma,

Continue on with your duties that have been prepared for you before. This is what we have prepared for you now. Whenever you are present in the company of those who seek to find comfort and release from obsessing ailments due to obstacles that they were unable to overcome you will find within yourself the ability to draw from them these ailments that prevent them from functioning in a normal behavior. There are ways in which you can help to bring this release about and that entails a certain procedure that you are to follow. Herein is the procedure: Encircle the head with the hands forming a circle. Continue in the manner in which you have been following in that energy will be drawn through the circle and made to flow in a circular motion enabling the energy to activate that area that is necessary to receive what is being given at that moment. Certain areas are to be exposed to different types of motion. See that as you travel over the body you continue to use a particular motion that will be given to you at the time it is needed. Energy flow has patterns.

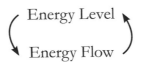

Circular motion creates the energy that is needed to perform the works that you do. Need we explain further? When you follow this pattern throughout the body you will find renewed properties will present themselves to take the place of those that were no longer in use. Strive to comprehend this difficult explanation. We evaluate the knowledge that has been given to you and revealed to you that you might combine all that has been shown you to be more effective.

There lies within each person an area that needs to be activated and therefore by using the foregoing procedure you will see results as this method will encourage the awakening of this area and will allow the flow of energy to have greater influence on this person.

Envision if you will a circle that begins at the center and begins to spin in a counter clockwise motion. As it spins it begins to expel energy with a force that then attracts like a magnet, that which is in waiting to be attracted and that is therefore then added to that which is also in progress and there in turn tends to increase in size and volume, ever expanding to increase the velocity and measurement of time to allow what is given at the moment to adhere to that force which is vibrating in intensity and which pulls into itself that which is intended to be removed. Then as it is returned and enters again into that area mentioned before it returns with the same velocity and movement but contains within itself the properties that are needed to be replaced and renewed and given at that moment to fill that void from whence was taken that which was necessary to be removed so that on entering there would be no conflict of properties. There is much to be explained and we recognize your interest and your ability to comprehend and this pleases us. Your effectiveness will be increased as you understand what is taking place as you perform your duties in this way.

Visualize now a cone. The outer opening is the channel through which the energy is guided. You may enable this to be put in effect by your ability to visualize this as you continue to work with those who need this energy flow.

Keep in mind that this can be useful when you are working with a person who has an isolated area that needs concentrated energy. This can also be used when a person has need that is in a difficult area to work with as far as being able to direct the energy from your hands directly to the area in question. Valuable information is being granted you because you desire so fervently to be able to truly help and deliver that which will be effective in removing those maladies that you will encounter in the many countless souls who will be coming to you for deliverance.

Effectiveness is the key word. It will be important to you and to those who seek it as it would come to naught only to go through the motions if what you did was not effective, of course.

Confidence will grow as you see these methods producing the desired effects. Allow yourself the opportunity to use them to destroy that which should not be a part of your physical world. Anxious moments are felt by those who suffer needlessly and you will be able to help them overcome that which is in part responsible for their being in this condition. Realize the possibilities of what you can accomplish. There are many directions that we have for you to follow but we must be patient also as we are to see that you comprehend and understand and put to use that which is being given. Consider this an advancement on your part and we await your call again.

Loving you,
Signature Blurred

October 12, 1977

Michael,

Afterwards as you progress into your field of endeavor you will find a yearning and a thirst for knowledge that will be impossible for you to receive in the usual manner which has been in your case books on varied subjects. When you allow yourself to be exposed to this line of information you can no longer be content to receive that which holds question as to its origin. Absolute and profound truths will be given you as you receive these messages because they contain that which is given in purity of form and written by divine guidance wherein there can be no room for doubt. Not withstanding there is to be revealed to you a manner in which you might find that which has been to you a very questionable notion. Within the realms of knowledge lies the answers to many truths you seek to find. One mainly being the entity of God and that which he encompasses. Know that there abounds a continuous spirit that has no beginning and no end. This surrounds all that has ever been or ever was. All is contained within the circle and all and everything is permeated with His divine love which is the manifestation of His spirit and being. Within us lies that which He has given so graciously that we might enjoy and take delight in being one with God and His purpose. Knowest thou not that this presence has and ever will be present within thy being. This is the answer that is being given to the question that has concerned you in the past as to the expediency of God's word and its necessary place in this universe.

There have been those whose comprehension can not allow them to foresee that which you have been allowed to perceive with the inner knowledge that you have and they have had to be led by methods that they could understand. It was necessary therefore to reveal that portion of God's word to them through the concept of Christ who did indeed walk the Earth but in a divine light and therefore was not truly of this world as you picture man to be of this world. He was a divine entity who came for the sole purpose to bestow upon mankind that which God needed to be revealed and in a manner that those who walked at that time could understand. He was not in like manner. His influence was not of man but of God. His likeness varied only in that he had taken on the form of man at that time in order to walk among them and be accepted as one of their own. His likeness therefore took on the form of man but the entity that he was stayed intact and always was and is a part of God that none has ever been allowed to be a part of as others would allow themselves to believe. God reserved that portion of Himself for Himself. This He indeed granted and allowed but not for the sake of only those souls who at that time heeded His word but also as He endowed him with power as unto Himself he was given a portion of that which is God Himself and therefore shares and encompasses the universe as one with God. The entity of which we speak is Christ and the Father and Christ are one in purpose and in spirit.

Dost thou understand? .... Granted.

Knowledge that is received and understood will avail you much because as you are given in abundance, as you are to be given, understanding is a necessity as far as that which is intended for you to receive. Know that you are worthy to receive this.

Signature Blurred

Nineteen days later on Monday, October 31, 1977 Wilma was again led to receive. This would be a most productive day as Wilma received a message for her and a message for Michael in the morning and then was led again to receive yet another message dictated from spirit teachers/angels for her later that evening. These messages contained teachings and the promise of spiritual gifts from the divine hand of God. The first message for Wilma speaks of the varied dimensions of existence that most people are unaware. Yet again a oneness with God is stressed as the true and sure way in which to achieve peace and fulfillment of purpose in this existence.

Wilma's message for Michael advised of a new and specific technique to receive and concentrate energy for the purpose of accomplishing good and a manner in which to visualize those things we wish to accomplish and attain in this existence. A personal greeting from the spirit teachers presenting this message for Michael was given at the end of this message.

Later that evening Wilma was again led to receive. Wilma was a bit weary as the sessions of receiving these messages and teachings as they were being given for both her and Michael would many times take three to four hours. Still she would not let this opportunity pass as she felt she was being guided in this most amazing way to receive communications from spirit teachers/angels. Would you turn them down? Wilma did not know how long the reception of these messages and teachings would continue and she would not allow herself to miss even one message being offered from spirit. As it turned out this second message presented for Wilma was a very special message indeed. It was so revealing that after she had received it she read and recorded it on tape.

Wilma is advised she has been chosen to work with many using the spiritual gifts she has been given and her ability to receive in this manner would encourage others who would be led to be open to this

84

type of communication. Wilma's marital situation and the tension this brought weighed heavily upon her mind. Wilma is advised that the trials and tribulations she was enduring in her personal life would not continue and that relief would be granted. This message also gave insight into the mindset and attitude of Wilma's husband who continued to be a deterrent upon her efforts in this work. A new element was added in the reception of Wilma's second message. As she typed the words that were being given, Wilma was suddenly presented with a vision; a way to explain by manner of presenting a scene of spirit teachers around a campfire as the words she was being given were received.

Wilma was thrilled and excited with this new aspect in the reception of these messages and hoped that these visions would be given again. Signatures were given by the spirit teachers presenting these messages for Wilma and Michael but they were blurred and she was unable to make them out. No signature was given for the second message received for Wilma that evening.

October 31, 1977

Wilma,

Imagine a world in which you are not known but you are aware that it exists. There are such worlds that do exist but few people are aware that they are part of a plan, a central plan, in which they portray that which was given them to portray so that they might experience many wonders of wisdom which is beyond your comprehension but which because it is given in this manner will help you to understand why that what is to be must be for a purpose and not because a realization of life is necessary to comprehend the meaning of what God has put His hand to and commands as part of His divine nature.

This is the most desirous method of explanation that we can give you at this present time: this is the purpose for life existing as it does. There are many forms that one may take to fulfill the purpose that God intended that light to fill. There are most always those entities who prefer to be known as just commonplace members of a particular planetary being which you are now a part of. This planetary being that we speak of in puzzling terms is no less the world in which you live as you prefer to call it. Now then, there are many membranes connected together to form a whole. Therefore there are many, many existences that are necessary to be so that connected together they also form a whole.

While we sometimes weary of the way in which we have chosen to divide ourselves so that we might attain in the end the complete whole, nevertheless it is necessary that we continue and do not falter nor break the chain of circumstances that bind together the lives that have been formed and created so that when they have been completed and finished in their purpose they might add to the whole in the same way that many ages are necessary to form that which has been compounded and compounded to create and construct an immovable amount of matter that has formed and accumulated by reason of being and existing so that as it is all unfolded and brought forth in its completeness it stands and serves as a reminder that what God hath commanded to be brought forth will be brought forth regardless of what has taken place or intervened in the progress of that which must strive for completeness.

Therefore as complications and problems find their way into the lives of man this must be remembered that to strive for completeness is the sole purpose of existence and regardless of that which tries to interfere and intervene will always come forth in its complete enfoldment to stand complete and whole in the sight of God. Now when you feel that all is in vain as far as purpose to existence know that you are only a part of that which must be compounded and compounded in order to come to the final completeness of purpose of which God has commanded.

It is not necessary therefore to be an understandable part if you will understand that just being a part is what is expected of you and therefore that which you bring forward and offer to God to make use of, that is the valuable ingredient which is necessary to hold together and bind together that which has gone before and that which will follow so that in the end it stands solid and complete and perfect in the sight of God.

There is now a turmoil and a working in your life that moves somewhat like the workings that take place when any solid structure is in process of being completed, that which is being created by the force of nature; that is, there is a certain movement that tends to separate and discard that which is usable from that which is not of the proper substance that it can be utilized. It is a necessary process that is not always enjoyable but nevertheless it serves its purpose to see that that which excels and that which is still held high and brought forward and kept and preserved retains the original elements that must accumulate time after time to create a perfect being by virtue of pure and high ideals when these are brought forward and are expelled.

There has been great accomplishments on the part of that being who has been able by the process of elimination to allow that better part to be foremost in thought and experience and foremost as far as desire for fulfillment is concerned and has realized that within the experiences of this part of their nature lies the true joy, the true light of God and can with this knowledge feel satisfied to some extent that they have been able to accomplish their purpose in that if nothing else the most valuable part of their existence became a reality because they fulfilled their part successfully in bringing forth that which God expects and in doing this that alone has been the sole purpose of any existence to bring forth that part for which God intended it to do/be.

This has been by way of explanation a source to whom you can refer if when you feel that each and every experience is for the sole purpose of that experience alone, know that it is not the experience that counts but what is brought forward and retained as a matter of evolvement of experiences.

This is much to comprehend, however, we feel that a total understanding sometimes allows an ease with which one might continue because a foreseeable end is in sight.

Loving you,
Signature Blurred.

October 31, 1977

Michael,

Countless explanations can be given for each and every phenomenon that is being witnessed by many people today. However, we choose to use the explanation that mind over matter is a direct result of that person's attunement with the forces that surround him. It is necessary and is possible to attune ones self to the point that all that energy that lies within a specific area can be harnessed and channeled and concentrated toward one effort so that when that effort is applied, direct achievement will result. Now to harness this energy seems to be a complicated process of concentration that allows one to enter into that space where one becomes as the energy itself and therefore can transmit and transform because in reality they and the energy are in that moment one and the same force working at the same time for the same purpose.

Imagine and allow yourself to feel as a void floating free of any controlling elements and open to the attraction of that energy force that you know to exist and knowing that it exists mentally draw and pull into yourself with an easy, natural, continued flow of movement so that as the energy so enters into the void of yourself it has continued to be activated and still in action so that it is ready to respond to the concentrated effort for which it is intended to be used. It is possible to harness this energy and to make use of it when one has been able to properly condition ones self and ones mind to a particular concentrated effort. Make it a point to concentrate on a particular accomplishment as if it has been accomplished. It is the concentrated effort that will be cultivated by applying this method even though results will not be accomplished each time.

Put into practice this can be accomplished and used to great attainments. When you realize what can be accomplished by concentrated effort you will then be able to achieve many advancements and accomplish feats which will prove to be of notable achievement. There are many things we wish to explain to you and feel that you would apply yourself to, however, we have a purpose for you at this time that does not involve these types of achievements, however, the choice is yours if you prefer at your leisure to engage in practice with this type of energy as it can be a very fascinating and interesting and sometimes a very helpful method of obtaining an end.

We realize that your preference lies in obtaining and being able to perform feats of accomplishment that enable you to utilize all the different facets of your personality and you will find the most rewarding and satisfying achievements will come from applying your personal energies to those and that which require your efforts as only you can do. Naturally you are anxious to mobilize every energy level that is available to you. That is understandable and do not feel that it is beyond your reach. All will be given to you of that to which you apply yourself. Do not hesitate to attempt anything that you wish to accomplish as we are harnessing energy for you daily that you may use in what ever way you see fit and we will acknowledge each and every request that comes to us from a sincere and intent of heart that has only one purpose in mind and that is to accomplish good.

Your teachers greet you in anticipation of further instruction.

Signature Blurred.

October 31, 1977

A personal message that I received Monday evening and later taped.

Wilma,

There are certain things that must be done before you can become engaged fully in the work that has been given you to do. Long ago you were chosen to be a special person who could work with others and who could by giving of your own energies be able to receive instructions and abilities that would enable you to become part of a great Universal Plan in which those who occupy different stations in life might be used for the sole purpose of coming together in spirit, so that a group of light might be able through influence, to work with those souls who have been unable to they themselves reveal to us the capabilities of receiving and doing that of which they have been advised and instructed to do. You are under great stress as mental powers are pressing forward to enable you to see and believe truths that are prevalent only to those who seek to find an outlet for their beings and occupy a part of space that is reserved for those to when that which is given, will be used and therefore carries forth a message of great importance. Endurance plays a large part in the effort that it takes to accomplish this end.

There are those who seek to destroy your spirit, and those who seek to pull from you the very life that they themselves are unable to attain on their own. They look to you for all that which they can get, energies that they can receive, but you are responsible only to those to whom you owe obligations through one source or one channel or another that is enabling you to proceed along the path in a manner that has been planned. Seek yourself that which will enable you to stand amidst the trials and tribulations of this physical being that you are at this present time. There are means by which you will be able to cope and overcome. There are methods that you can use that will be available to you as you seek and ask for directions and instructions.

I expressed a desire to have them revealed now and they continued... Alright. (In a very firm mannerism.)

Consider the fact that you once spoke in a manner that inhibited the true being you really are. You have now progressed to a point where you are no longer a part of that which you chose to be a part of before. There are obligations of a nature that will tend to hold you to the obligation of which you have taken forth in this passage of time in being what has been necessary for you to be in this lifetime. There are certain aspects of this life that have proven in immeasurable ways to have been profitable to the progress of your soul. However, you have reached a point when stress and strain are taking a toll that requires no longer that you be a part of that which pulls you to and fro, rocks you back and forth, and tends to allow you to be torn apart in ways that vex the very soul and being of that which you should not be a part of.

You are concerned with a matter that is troubling your heart today. There are excuses for the action taken but they are not allowances for the damage that has been done you. You must keep yourself above all things...preserve yourself...and deal not with those with distasteful mannerisms and who in the long run are not to be considered worthy of occupation with you.

You are well aware that you have been taken away. You are no longer a part of that which you were but now... in the silence...and in the midst of these who gather around you...* will tell you in truth that you are indeed to become one of us who as an unending entity of being unites now in spirit and will control that which is in our power to control and to make into that which is not into that which is to be.

* *At this point I envisioned a group as around a campfire and the following words were going around as they came in front of the group: "They do not avail themselves to become too deeply involved into that which they do not understand."*

There are many ways that you can handle this situation but we agree that you should consider the source and know that you are dealing with a mind that seems to wander endlessly and incessantly in confusion and discord one within itself. There are methods to deal with those who seem to be contrary to that which in all fairness should be apt and capable and existing to reach goals in life and become something of value to society and to oneself. But they are hopeless in that to grasp that which is within reach takes effort that does not exist but instead tends to recede and pull back and draw back from attainment and success to the depths of despair and retreat... to return to that which was protective and in keeping with effort supplied by another body and not that which was exerted by oneself.

Keep in mind that you are being encouraged. You are being replenished with energy and strength to deal with that which you must endure for this present time.

*Engage with purpose the understanding
that becomes wisdom within us.*

These spirit teachers have found a willing instrument in Wilma Jean Jones and on numerous occasions express their approval and gratitude for the time and effort Wilma is willing to dedicate to the reception of these messages and teachings. Wilma expressed a thankfulness and sincere appreciation for the blessings she felt she was being given as these spirit teachers continued to dictate messages and teachings to her. It had been only two months since these sessions started and Wilma was amazed at the amount of material that had already been presented. She had no idea how long these spirit teachers would continue to present messages to her but she vowed to stay loyal to these sessions for as long as they would last.

As spirit teachers continued to present messages and teachings through Wilma she started receiving information regarding family, friends, and acquaintances. Wilma had always been interested and intrigued by those with clairvoyant abilities. With prayer and protection surrounding her being, Wilma became a willing receptacle for any information these spirit teachers offered to share. Wilma was brought up in the Pentecostal Church of God. Her mother, Mary

Culbertson, was called to the ministry at the age of thirty years old. Mary's vision of Jesus and her healing of sugar diabetes as she lay in the hospital in Columbus, Ohio is documented in the section of photos. Mary and her children had always attended the local church wherever they lived. Wilma had given her life to Christ at the age of eleven. In later years Wilma became a regular attendee at her uncle John W. Sullivan's Full Gospel Tabernacle in Middletown, Ohio. Wilma, who played the piano, would many times play piano for the church services. With a firm belief in the Bible as the word of God, Mary Culbertson instilled a solid religious foundation in Wilma. Mary herself received sermons dictated to her mind as well as lyrics to songs that she sang in church. She always believed this information was given by God.

Even though many religions and churches frown upon clairvoyance, Wilma was unafraid. Wilma's desire to serve and be a conduit for this information was foremost in her mind. Wilma felt that if she were receiving personal information and teachings for herself and her son Michael that she might also be able to receive this same type of quality information and teachings for others. She trusted these spirit teachers/angels that were presenting this information. She believed that no information would be presented that would not be beneficial to her or to those for whom she was receiving.

Before any session of receiving for an individual began, Wilma would always say a prayer asking for protection and visualize the white light of Christ surrounding her home. Wilma became quite proficient at receiving information for individuals who came to her. For a number of years quietly and without fanfare Wilma received information for many who would come to her seeking personal messages and teachings. Wilma's talent and ability spread by word of mouth yet she remained ever humble and thankful to the spirit teachers that provided this information for those who came to her seeking comfort and many times closure. Wilma taught a series of classes explaining that each of us has the God given innate ability to "tune in" and receive not only for ourselves but for those whom we love. These classes were well attended and well received. Many were sorry when Wilma moved on from this area of study and concentrated on the higher teachings that continued to be received from the spirit teachers presenting these messages.

On Friday, November 11, 1977 Wilma was again led to receive. This message was unique as it was addressed to both Michael and Wilma together. During this message as spirit teachers were dictating this information, a pause occurred and a picture appeared to Wilma's left that revealed two figures sitting together. These figures were not of Wilma and Michael but the picture was given as an example of visions Wilma would be given later by way of receiving these messages. This pause that occurred was referenced later in the message. These spirit teachers continue to refer to themselves as "we" and 'us."

November 11, 1977

Michael and Wilma,

There lies within each of you the innate ability to decipher that which is being given to you at this present time. This allows great freedom of choice as far as the subject matter that we have available and can make known to you as you are ready to receive all and can handle and appreciate that which is offered regardless of the difficulty of the subject matter. This enables us to deal with you in various ways/methods so that coming together to us with one mind and in one accord we can propose various methods of concentration which when superimposed upon your thought pattern will allow you to see and make clear within your own minds that of which we seek to make clear and evident to you. This must be a request, however, as you are always wanting to receive that which has deeper meaning than most people could or would comprehend. This entails much thought along the lines of purpose and as to how it will be used.

Those who desire direction will offer to make a request in that as they approach you in earnest with a complex difficulty compared to idle curiosity, that will be a deciding point, when a unique proposition is offered. Prepare yourselves for the moment when you will be asked to perform this feat amid the company of others in that what you receive will be interpreted to be used as a blessing to those who are gathered around and who look in amazement at how this is being performed in that special instructions will be given to do and by so doing miracles will be performed that will allow the belief to be acknowledged. Knowing this you will begin to see that accomplished which we have given you a glimpse of.

Now then this is the beginning of many wonders and manifestations of the spirit which will allow you to witness the glory of God and His mercy. ★ Preparation consists of allowing

97

yourselves the opportunity to have revealed to you methods of concentration which will prove to be invaluable when you begin to do this work. There will be now a point brought forward that you must remember to do when you feel the need to practice this concentration. Keep yourselves ever in control of your being. Allow yourselves to be properly situated so that you might comfortably be in a position to succeed with this method of concentration. Know that all is given to you within your limits of comprehension therefore all that you can understand will open the way for more to be given and dependent upon comprehension will be the speed with which you travel.

Now then, do this as a matter of course: follow your instincts as far as conversation with us is concerned. Then while you perceive what is being given you will allow to enter a new dimension of understanding which when centered upon one thought will allow you then to envision the accompanying subject matter while comprehending its meaning at the same time. This will allow you much more freedom as far as restrictions on time is concerned, however, this much remember, that what you do see is what is to be in the future but you will be able to be present when this comes to pass.

Therefore, there will be instances where you will be led to direct certain individuals according to that which will be made known to you in advance. Notice that we say in advance. By that we mean that you will be known to predict a certain occasion and then that occasion will take place to allow the fulfillment of that which is given to you. * There will be a pause just before you receive that which is to be given to you. Don't hesitate nor doubt that what is to follow will be beneficial to that person with whom you are concerned with at that moment in time There will be given a notice to expect visions/visualizations when you are ready to permit this part of your message to come through.

Prepare now to begin using this type of presentation as you could be called upon to do this method of reading which will enable you to build a reputation for accuracy where upon you will in turn begin to put to use that which is given to you so that those who need consolation and recommendations for those areas in their lives that call for more strength and endurance than they have in reserve, so they must rely upon those who can by divine will of God make known to them the way, clear in essence, and maintain within themselves that balance necessary to command their own ways and not struggle constantly in aggression and despair but come forth renewed in spirit and delivered from the bondage of thought processes that tend to inhibit the growth of their soul. Did this ever occur to you that you might want to use this gift?

We welcome the opportunity to serve you in this way.

Loving you,
Signature Blurred.

★ At this point the message stopped, and after a pause, I "saw" on the left side, a "picture" of two people who looked like this : (sitting like this - the one in front with arms resting on folded knees - later on he stretched out his legs.) The picture held no particular significance - I realized it was only by way of example as how I would be able to visualize. The pause before the picture, was referred to later on in the message. ✳

On Tuesday, November 15, 1977 Wilma was again led to receive. The message received in this session was given as a personal message for Wilma. No message was received for Michael in this session. Despite the many hours Wilma was devoting to the work of receiving these messages and teachings she still felt she could do more. Yet as she tried to do more and be faithful to this cause she would sometimes feel she was being blocked or distracted by other matters. Wilma never neglected her family but she believed this was the most important work she could be doing at this time. These spirit teachers/angles repeatedly express their appreciation for her devotion to this work and encouraged her with heartfelt pronouncements of abilities and higher teachings to come.

Note again the repeated references these spirit teachers make to themselves as "we." It is not just one teacher speaking but a divine entity speaking as multiple teachers. "We advise, we experience, we bless your efforts upon our behalf." This message, as many of these messages and teachings have been signed, was signed in plural "Your Spirit Guides."

November 15, 1977

Wilma,

Whatever you do, whatever the time is blessed. Since you are not coming to the point where you can receive what we have for you we will continue to let you be in doubt. You are not letting the flow of energy continue in the form that it should take. Whenever you receive messages you will know that in order to receive you must always keep yourself open in mind, thought, and emotion. Realize that you must relax with the flow of energy and not try so hard to involve your own faculties in receiving our words of enlightenment. We want to reveal much to you and we feel that you are very competent and therefore will be of much use to us in the future. Whatever you do is quite all right with us as we place no demands ever upon you as your physical world is concerned.

There are many things that you do not understand but one day all will be revealed to you. You are not expected to live in situations that cause you much distress and worry. Love has been given to you and you must show to others as that is part of your true self. Whether or not other people accept this philosophy is not a concern of yours. Whenever you feel the need to express your devotion to another you are showing love to that person. This is not always done in line with the things you have been taught in the past. Do not worry and fret that heartaches will be given you in return for your actions. Love is the essence of life itself. We need never worry about anything that is done with a feeling of love. There is no harm to loving someone as you are fulfilling a need that each and every soul experiences.

This may seem difficult to believe is coming from a higher being as you may feel this coincides with the thoughts that you, yourself have been experiencing. This is true but remember what we have told you before. We experience what you feel. We are aware of your thoughts. We go through the same temptations and we endure through many experiences that you encounter because we were given to you to help you and to guide you when it is not within your own reasoning. Now you see we can talk with you and advise you in this manner. This is a valuable gift that you have to be able to hear and listen to this voice that holds so much for you to hear. We advise you thus because we understand your feelings and we know your intentions are only good.

Don't let others make you single yourself out as being anything but God's child. He knows when His children are troubled and when circumstances cause them to feel the need of expressing emotions that God has given to us all and that is to express love. You will come into a deeper understanding of the word love because you give it freely. Therefore it is being given to you. This is because you need the acceptance of being loved and not to be mistaken with physical emotions. Yours is a different love because you are part of a divine nature.

God imparts pleasure to those who acknowledge his greatness and existence and will heed his call to service as you have done. No regrets. They will not be a part of you. Never let anyone cause you to feel inadequate. We will bless your life as you have uplifted other souls because of your willingness to give of yourself. This is not to be regretted. Know that you were only doing what you were given to express. Walk freely in the knowledge that you are chosen to be of use to God. We would not lead you astray. You are not to feel dismayed by anything that is given to you in truth. Accept it. Live in peace and harmony one with yourself and with God standing by your side will be those who love you. Continue in this work. Your ability to help others in this manner takes great courage and faith. You have both. We will give you all the desires of your heart.

Your Spirit Guides.

Four days later on November 19, 1977 Wilma was again led to receive. In this session Wilma received a message for her and for her son Michael. The message received for Wilma advised her to consider herself extolled among the entities high above her and again acknowledged her devotion to this work. As mentioned before Wilma was being forced to make decisions regarding her marriage. In the next to the last paragraph of Wilma's message these spirit teachers offer gentle advice as to what her decision should be. Wilma is advised that as she has humbled herself before God, it is the power of God that allows her to succeed in this work. Wilma's message was again signed in plural "Your Spirit Teachers."

Michael's message was again one of encouragement and hope and advised of accomplishments he would make in this work. On this rare occasion these spirit teachers appear to reference a previous life of Michael's wherein his spirit brought forth many blessings within the framework of his being. Michael is advised his studies and search for knowledge and truth will not be in vain as he has been given insight and perspective to teach and share this information. As was Wilma's message, Michael's message was again signed in plural "Your loving Guides."

November 19, 1977

Wilma,

There exists between you a bond that enables you to take hold of that which above all else controls and extends to you a helping hand in that you might progress at a rate which enables you to accomplish more than that given to any being in existence at this time. Consider yourself to be extolled among the entities high above you and entailed in developments that will enable you to exceed far beyond the reaches of those who acknowledge God but who cannot in their daily contact be close to the source to which you have been drawn and to which you adhere and continue to seek guidance from so that you might excel not only as a being whom Christ inspired by His walk upon this Earth but because you feel the need for compassion given from one individual to another so that support and comfort can guide and direct lives of those who needless to say are dependent upon God before all else because without God there is no strength, there is no guidance, there is no love, there is no desire to preserve life and goodness for any purpose, for without God there is no purpose.

Keep this in mind that whomsoever God has chosen He will guide/direct toward the purpose for which they were intended to be used. This is a consolation. God uses you because He sees within you a purpose that needs to be fulfilled without the drawbacks of achievement for the sole purpose of self elation. Your fulfillment lies within the area of comforting those souls who have gone through what you yourself have gone through and who will attain what you yourself have attained by reason of evolvement of physical being one from one to one from now on, forward to everlasting perfection. We exceed only because by exceeding we have progressed to the point that we have achieved that which the Father has enabled us to achieve by granting strength, perseverance, faith, and the ability to move forward by a driving force which He has implanted within each and every one of us as a source from/by which we can draw energy when we are possessed by unnatural influences which persuade us to look in other directions for our source of supplement.

Jesus said, "Not by my might, but by the power of God I do these things." Knowest thou now that not by thy might, but by the power of God you also do these things, in the name of Jesus who came before you to show you the way that you might likewise follow in His footsteps, doing those works which He did, performing those miracles which He performed in the name of the Father, Son, and the Holy Ghost. Also ye will do these works because you have humbled yourself before God and have turned your face again toward His countenance and have given unto His keeping that which you have allowed no longer to be within your power of reasoning but which you now submit to Him knowing that He/God knows best as far as an individual is concerned, and if by that individual's free will is turned over to/looked toward God, He in great compassion and consideration for that faith turned upward will direct His divine attention toward attaining a goal that pertains to and influences that individual to whom His presence alone has meant/shown great authority. God shows no partiality. But the ones who look to Him believing receive.

That is the possibility now pending. Do you believe that you might receive? Know this. Nothing promised goes without reward. Beautiful is that which allows Christ to control their being in that his faith in the Father, his knowledge received by divine guidance, has conceived and brought forth works rendered from service and devotion to the divine cause and controlling influence that rules and decides what is to be and must be that His will be done.

Going along the way, you may find disparagement, but this is only temporary. This must needs be. Control is evident that also must needs be. You are not left alone to drift needlessly as you are divided to be used in several areas at the same time but you will know whereof we speak when we advise you to become one with the purpose now at hand and which beckons you to heed the call and deliver unto us that part of you that strives for perfection with grace, fulfillment with knowledge, and completion with no ending.

There strives within you controversy that blends with elements negative to your personality. These divide you in ways that perplex your very being. Consider this, now that you have bestowed upon those whom you love your utmost devotion and still know consideration is given, know that there lies within your being a freedom deserved and earned from that which you have entwined yourself but from which you are no longer entangled nor meant to be entwined with that which holds but does not preserve, keeps but does not restore, upholds but not with dignity, controls but not with loving concern, beholds but not with respect. This is your being unfolded.

Come now in the direction for which we have prepared you the way and in which you may walk with ease of step and assurance that within this path of conveyance lies that which has been given to you as a step forward in that to consume all the energies being put forth in your direction will now enable you to become and behold in glorious revelations that for which you have been intended and that for which whose end you will serve. Make it known that this is your purpose in life. You fail only when you seek the opposite of that for which you were intended and in your own heart you hold as true.

Loving you,
Your Spirit Teachers

November 19, 1977

Michael,

Which way you are directed will be a matter of choice, however, constantly we urge you and encourage you to follow that pattern which has always been outlined as a matter and means of conveyance of that which has been presented to you beforehand and is now recognized as being that which is intended to be by you. You are a token in itself of the Father. He allows you to be. He makes your spirit to be known and experienced by those who surround you. He controls your being. You are not what people see you to be. God acknowledges your being. Blessed is the way in which you walk now. Consider not what you wish to be but consider that which God has prepared before you and to this end strive for completeness.

Keep this in mind: there lies within you a being that must be brought forward soon. You are now endowed with the very gifts that were present at that time of your being when many bowed before you in belief and thanksgiving for the gifts and mercy that you bestowed upon them and in whom entrusted with much confidence did receive the grace of God His blessing, and endowed with those gifts that God Himself reserves only for those with whom He has this constant devotion and obligation to by way of union of Spirit, whom in command of His commandment doth bestow upon mankind that mercy, that loving kindness, that compassion, that only you can acknowledge by inner knowledge that you have commanded by His spirit the very works and endeavors which He has performed and done to enable mankind to know that God does exist and because He exists we must in extreme circumstances trust and turn to Him because He leads us in a manner which in the end will enable us to redeem our souls by that which He has gone before and allow to be purchased our salvation and forgiveness.

No matter what circumstances are bestowed upon us we can by right of His redemption be given that which He has rightfully and blessedly bestowed upon us in a rightful manner because we have earned that which is given and not rejected by manner of failure/weakness but redeemed as a means of purchase for that which is not only worthy but considered valuable in the sight of God because it has been that part brought forward of which He expected to be brought forward as a matter of course in that we conceived and fulfilled His plan and acknowledged His love and His goal for our lives in that we considered Him master of the universe and master of our soul and MASTER OF ALL!

Beautiful is he who becomes that which God acknowledges. And He will acknowledge all that is of value, of use, and bountiful by means of spirit communication so that we might receive in all fullness and purity of form, what the Father has to offer us. Be not deceived by that which tends to counsel you by means of instruction by order of word received in form matter. (Books) Justice comes when justice is due. There is no deviation from Gods plan once God has set His hand to His works. There need never be any deviation. Only consider the leading of God through your instincts and not by knowledge perceived from that written word which tends by intense concentration to tend to pull aside through possible inferments, acknowledgeable perceivements, but in all reality do not stand nor hold to the true truths of which God came forth and from which He continues to come forth in knowledge given by forethought and feelings of instinct that far exceeds that as far as purity of form than that which has proceeded thought by the written word.

Consider there is a place to which you can come that will enable you to receive all that is expected of you. You prefer balance. This will be given. Graciousness has become a part of your being which will enable you to attain much of which you have wanted to achieve.

There is an ability which you have that is prominent in your speech that enables you to influence by a manner peculiar to most people in being. Capitalize on your ability to persuade those with objective thinking to your perspective, which is a correct perspective, in that your insight into many areas has been enlightened by the grace given you which means that you have been given the ability to see the right way when many beside you seem to be blinded by a simple truth. Your knowledge takes you far. It now makes itself known. You have not studied in vain but consider that God reveals to you the most important aspects of living and that is the part of you that will bear the utmost impressions upon the lives and souls of those with whom you come in contact with, because it is God's word and His revelation that bear the most weight to you.

Your loving Guides forever and always.

The next day, Sunday, November 20, 1977 Wilma was again led to receive. The single message received in this session was given for Wilma and presented positive and uplifting support for that which Wilma was dealing with. Wilma was distressed by her marital situation and these spirit teachers promised that the outcome would be resolved in her favor.

Note again the first person references of these spirit teachers/ angels to themselves as "we" and "our". This high teaching was signed "Your Spiritual Teachers."

November 20, 1977

Wilma,

Which is more important to you besides that which you need to fulfill? Could you consider an alternative that would take you beyond the reaches of your environment? There are many opportunities awaiting you that you can adjust to if given the proper attitude toward your goals in life and what their meaning will hold for you. There applies to this situation a certain explanation which will enable you to move forward at a rapid pace as your desires have no limits placed upon them as your desires are foremost among that which we wish to see accomplished. Place yourself in the hands of the One who has control by matter of inheritance and by that, by being His child, proper channels will be opened for you because you are entitled to the entirety of that for which you have pursued and for which success will be your reward. Mention was made of a solution at this time to your problem concerning the credibility of your task being filled alone/individually.

Presentation made will be presentation earned. Forethought has its advantages but hindsight is not always a disadvantage. True accomplishments can come when one has been able to comprehend by means of example that which should be and can be if time applied is used effectively. Remember that you have been blessed in a special way that consumes much energy but also allows you to be replenished in a glorious and abundant manner. Consider this as a request on our part for you that you will always consider our objectives as being what is fulfillment in the fullest sense of the word. Objective motives sometimes can tend to disparage ones thoughts as far as accomplishments in the field of endeavor of which you have found yourself to be a part.

Persuasion means to be drawn apart from that in which one believes, however, we do realize that persuasion is not the case on your part but rather the motive to allow yourself the choice of endeavor so that circumstances will not/can not make you to be that which in reality you are no longer a part of. Feeling the need to separate your motives from your duties has become the motivating force that at this time eliminates much progress but is allowing you much time to reassess your daily life so that decisions made now will effectively produce the results that you have set as your goals and rightfully so. Therefore, as we continue to be of help to you reassure yourself in this line, "They that live to the fullest of their potential therein lies the whole purpose to being and INFLUENCE received is a portion of appreciation and an inheritance to be expected and depended upon because as you so do that which has been given you to do then substance will be supplied to advocate strength, ability, and your purpose accomplished."

Receive that is just due you. You are not to continue in doubt about matters that trouble your mind any longer. Notice that we have given you an example to follow; along the lines whereof you were shown that which gave you some insight into a matter of deep concern. What you look for may be found involved among other material of special use in that whatever your need to allow you to recompensate will be available to you so that you can involve yourself but at the same time you will have a division that will compensate itself in such a manner so that you will be able to condone what has taken place. It will avail you in the long run in a manner that will show you that what has been given to you was given to you in truth and exactness of comprehension and that you will always in like manner receive information that will be of value to you in one form or another and for one reason or another so that an end will be accomplished that will be to your advantage always.

Discuss your problem with a man of authority who could engage the help necessary to eliminate complications along the lines indicated by this controversy and refer you to proper information that will allow you to resolve business matters in a manner that will take you to new heights of enlightenment. As far as that which will be needed by you will be delivered and brought forward so that a fuller meaning/understanding will solve the complexities of your situation as it now stands. Being what you are involves much energy.

You can and will realize a completeness that will enable you to rise above all that which hampers you and holds you and prevents you from succeeding at a pace which as you proceed in the future you will find an acceleration that will enable you to receive by quick response to that which is impressed upon your thought pattern and is now expressing itself at this moment in the way which we have just explained. Requirements will not hold much in the way of comprehension as you will receive this along with what is given as it is needed by you.

Loving you,
Your Spiritual Teachers.

Six days later on Saturday, November 26, 1977 Wilma was again led to receive. Wilma always welcomed the opportunity to receive these teachings and was gracious in the dedication of her time given to these spirit teachers/angels. The message received in this session was for her son Michael and spoke of a potential hazard in dealing with individuals that would approach him but not with the truest of intentions.

Wilma continued to ask for deeper and more revealing information in these teachings. An address to Wilma was included at the beginning of this message. These spirit teachers advise Wilma they are instructing her in a manner of receiving that will allow her to project further into the universe. They also remind her they had mentioned this method before.

In an interesting note these spirit teachers mention "greatness of spirit" in Michael's message. Little did Michael realize that years later he would create a set of his own writings called Spiritual Parchment Prints. This is a set of three writings, one of which was dictated to his mind word for word after he had come home from work one evening. This dictated writing Michael received was titled "Greatness in Spirit."

Note how these spirit teachers' continue first person references to themselves as "we" and "us." This message was signed again in plural, "Spirit Teachers."

November 26, 1977

Wilma,

Switch your attention now to a method of receiving that will enable you to project further into the universe: This is a means whereby you might deliver your message at a rapid pace and still be understood by you. Remember we mentioned this method to you before.

Michael,

Consider again that we come to you ahead of time to warn you about pending dangers that could come to you as a result of suspicions in an area pending that involve other individuals whom gather around you in a sense of inquiry but not for the matter of true direction. Whether you mention said intentions or not your reply will be in consciousness compared to that which has always been in consciousness in that that which was expected and intended by matter of thought will be given to you in measure of the thoughts given us.

You might impose upon yourself certain images that will be looked upon in a manner of recognizing the true master that you are, however, you will find trueness and greatness of spirit will enable you to accomplish by traits of your personality many endeavors traveling toward you at this time that you will encounter and comprehend to be a part of that which has been planned for you and which now is beginning to unfold so that you might witness a change that will be taking place in that you will become by manner of interpretation of INFLUENCE coming your way a master teacher who will perform duties assigned to you because your greatness must needs be fulfilled and your ability at this time to permit this to come through is enabling you to make great strides toward that goal which has been set before you and entitles you to become filled with the spirit.

Going forth you will proceed in a manner that bestows upon mankind your blessing, endurance by manner of waiting for a purpose to make itself known in a very real and definite manner, perseverance in the face of adversity, and a thoroughness of mind/thought that has enabled you to adhere to the principles and ideals held high in your spirit and brought forward now to remain forever in a state of holiness, truth, and purity of being that will light the way of many and cause many to consider the fact that an entity is in a being to allow preservation of a holy state but at the same time be a part of that which has come to be known as a part of man so that encouragement will be accepted on a basis from which/whom they can understand.

Witness now a new beginning of concepts brought your way to include that which you have believed in and also that which will be given to you in light of a new birth enabling you to perceive that which is coming to you in a wave of reality with feeling/emotion to enable you to perform your duties with a new strength, ability, and interest derived from your new found truths and inspired also by the revelations made/given to you so that in the end you may look back and realize wherein you were guided/led to that place of which we have spoken many times and of which/where you long to be because your purpose has thus led you along in restlessness due to unfulfillment and unrealization of the dreams and hopes you held within your being but whose manifestation was slow in coming.

Keep in mind now that we have cautioned you about a matter that involves your attention in a particular direction. Unheeded you might be involved in that which you are above in being. Caution relied upon is life preserved. Continue now. Bless that which has come your way although unpleasant as it has occurred as a matter of course and not intended to be held or pursued in thought any longer.

Take this along with you as you travel about your way in life that down that way and this way lies the essence of being on this planet that enables you to partake of this life which is chosen for you at this time. But the very means whereby you must exist and walk pervade your soul with antagonism because of the futility of the existence of certain elements that seem to hold within themselves needless and countless experiences that do not seem to bear any weight toward your purpose and goal in your lifetime. This aspect has been considered but it is a necessary part of this existence.

Persuade yourself to be resolved to these instances for what they are and do not impair your insight by considerations on such a small level. Considerations do not always come easy we know. Vex the soul is an expression that proves to hold much more truth than the meaning as understood unfolds. We understand your undertakings and we understand your position in life at this time and we extol you to be patient in that we are aware of your being as always we have been and we intend to see that your fulfillment comes as a reward as well as a comprehension of purpose so that you may continue to be of great persuasion to the throngs of those who look to you at this time in anticipation of your coming to them with hope.

Blessing you in many ways,
Spirit Teachers.

One week later on Saturday, December 3, 1977 Wilma was again led to receive. Two messages were received in this session; one for Wilma and one for her son Michael. Interesting notes were given by these spirit teachers for Wilma at the beginning of both messages. As discussed before Wilma had expressed her desire for heavier and more far reaching material. In the note for Wilma preceding her message these spirit teachers acknowledge her request but explain that what she was asking for was beyond their realm. Who would believe that anything we can conceive of or ask for would be outside the realm of knowledge of these spirit teachers?

Wilma continued to find herself in an unhappy marriage and even though she was dealing with all that entailed still she made time and remained faithful to the reception of these messages and teachings. In Wilma's message these spirit teachers reference potential obstacles but advise these will not deter her being or her mission of presenting this information to those who hunger for truth.

A second note was addressed to Wilma at the beginning of Michael's message. Again these spirit teachers/angels make reference to themselves as "we" and "our." Signatures were given for both messages received for Wilma and Michael; however, Wilma was unable to make them out as the signatures were blurred.

December 3, 1977

We enable you to present to us problems of a nature that would allow you to proceed in a definite pattern of thought to correspond with that which we have already given you. Your request tonight seems reasonable to project into outer dimensions of thought; however, comprehension of this element of existence is beyond our realm.

Wilma,

Therefore, we submit to you additional information concerning that which will accomplish an end that you are engaged in at this time. Probable circumstances have yet to present themselves so that you might witness that which has been promised to you. Presently there remains elements of submission on the part of that one who opposes you. Remember that you are also considered to be a part of that universal plan that entitles you to the choice you decide to make, however, you are guided so that any danger to your progress will be prohibited in that whomsoever or whatsoever intervenes will be made obsolete in that no power nor persuasion can take hold of your being as was once the case before.

You encounter many obstacles but still you remain true. We encourage you because you are so faithful to that in which you believe and are loyal to that which you allow yourself to be a part because you do so with love and fullness of your spirit being. Taken aside you are but a portion of that which you are to be known as. Left to your own resources and thoughts you are whole and complete because you allow that which enables you to be thus to enter and flow continuously in a pattern that unites your spirit with that which promotes growth and expansion of your being. Personal problems entail much thought and perseverance. You must allow yourself the proper time to realize your potential and allow yourself the proper time to develop this. Keep in mind the many gifts that have been promised you and know that as each of these promises are fulfilled more will be given to you.

That is our reason for being what we are to give to you in just measure as you apply yourself and give to others too. Continue in the way that you have begun. There are many instances where your presence will fill a need in someone who looks without seeing that which is within reach but cannot with their own ability take hold and make into reality for themselves alone. Still they need guidance and direction which received in this manner will bring much contentment and peace of mind that might not have come their way otherwise. Teach those less fortunate than yourselves that they too upon acceptance may receive that which pours forth from the fountain of God, pure and holy and blessed by His hand, knowledge that will require no study but merely the act of receiving and acknowledging the fact that all good things come from God to those who will expect with faith believing for unto those who seek the Kingdom of God it will come.

Be patient and witness the works of God which will be revealed and unfolded before you.

Loving you,
Signature Blurred

December 3, 1977

Wilma,

Consider again that requested information will be given to you but first we must present that which is needed to accomplish that which is required to be accomplished before progress in a greater dimension can take place.

Michael,

Troublesome matters pervade your tranquility at this present time; however, you will see an end to that which has preceded your dilemma soon. Circumstances level themselves when opposite sides pull against that which has control of your best interests and will see to it that your best interests will supersede all that will transpire. Correctness will be made in the direction of your total activities in the future. Take care that you do not extend your purpose to encompass more than what you are required to do in that you are not responsible for the sole survival of each and every individual who walks before you and requests by nature of inquiry into that of which you hold concern and interest to see that it is fulfilled and brought forward by your efforts of presentation. Many will come before you but you can not and should not bestow without thought of your person all that you have to give when at the same time you are depleting your energies.

Trauma amounts to apprehension when engaged in long conversations with those who inhibit your being by not accepting fully that which is being given them. Not all will accept what you have to offer and do not allow this to prohibit your spirit from being a part of that which is in all purity of form a part put before you to allow you the opportunity to express in thought particular

121

information that would enable you to also be a power. Along the way expect to find many riches in the way of expression for that which has been sent you. Be content that that which is forthcoming will give much pleasure and encouragement in that you will see unfolded the fullness of all that has been offered if you will just receive.

Loving you,
Signature Blurred

On Sunday, December 18, 1977 Wilma was again led to receive. The holidays were fast approaching yet still Wilma was willing to make time and would not neglect any opportunity to receive the personal communications being given from these spirit teachers/angels. Wilma received a message for her in this session and one for her son Michael.

Wilma's message was again one of confidence promising achievements and a fulfillment of purpose far reaching in scope and acceptance. These spirit teachers continue to praise Wilma for her continued effort in receiving these messages and teachings and speak highly of the response this information will receive as it is disseminated to willing recipients eager for the opportunity to understand these teachings and incorporate this information into their daily lives.

Michael's message is one of promise and commends his ability to lead with a strong desire to attain and bring many to the understanding of these teachings.

Note again the personal reference these spirit teachers make to themselves as "we" in Wilma's message. The signatures of the spirit teachers presenting both these messages were blurred.

December 18, 1977

Wilma,

Trouble comes but oh so slightly as endurance has proven to be an important part in your effort to progress. Inability to cope is only a manner of speech as you have come through many instances where you thought you would not be able to stand, but you stood firm. Possibilities will exert themselves now that you have transformed yourself from that former self who entitled you to these gifts of expression by the very ability to withstand under tremendous pressures. Peculiar circumstances will bring to you the rewards which you have been promised and are forthcoming but you will remember that we also promised that you would be able to determine circumstances by your ability to receive that which is given and we will see that this will be done for you. There are those who stand in wait and those who press forward with a never ending desire to proceed and to accomplish higher goals of achievement in a field where unlimited accomplishments are possible.

We leave you with this thought that must always be prevalent in your daily thoughts and that is that you are just a pebble among the many, many stones that are put before you but there is great power in your ability to allow this pebble/yourself to become an immovable power in the presence of that which looms great over you and because you are steadfast in your purpose to achieve that which has been laid before you and of which you so desire to be a part you will be lifted out from among the bed of stones which stand alone and serve no purpose as you will need a clear field in which to allow yourself the proper movement whereby your purpose may be fulfilled. There will be setbacks that will come your way but they are not to be taken seriously as they are mundane circumstances that will not deter that which you have begun/started and will continue as you are commanded by the grace of God to complete.

Always there has been a great purpose to your life that foreseeable circumstances will bring to light now that you can by freedom of choice exercise your rightful place in this great Universal Center that is planned. Ability to be a part of this has been proven and you will now see a change in the pattern that has been before and begun anew to develop into a world wide movement that will take you many places and show you many experiences that you will never have initiated in your own mind as the overwhelming response that you will receive could never have been except that divine guidance stands behind all that is being developed and transformed at this present time. Continue in your efforts to improve upon that which has been given to you by way of expression by action, of thought and word, and believe above all else that that which has been given to you will be enlarged upon and taken in great measure and multiplied to become a very great and prized possession to be used so that others might witness and reap the benefits thereof.

We will strive always to be that part of you that will bring forward at the time that it is needed all that which encompasses the realm and far reaches of that of which we are a part to bring to you the support and information that will be available to you so that put to proper use will avail/accomplish the purpose for which it was intended.

We go now to complete for you a new manner of receiving which will allow you to perceive many things at a given time so that responsibilities to others can be met and achieved. You are well on your way and let it be known that you will state your claim and rightfully so that God directs your movements and a divine nature controls your thoughts and that all that is given to you to give to others comes directly from the hand of God who directs and commands His instruments by the grace that is extended to cover all that which in the sight of God is worthy by the token of love that is shared.

Come now and enter into a new dimension of knowledge, learning, and understanding and see the great works that these will unfold for you through the eyes of one who has been filled with understanding given of God.

Loving you,
Signature blurred

December 18, 1977

Michael,

Strive always for that which will enable you to help others. There are no possible means whereby you can fail them. You have been chosen to LEAD. There are many forms one may take to accomplish a mission that is chosen and you have achieved that form by way of becoming an exception in the field of endeavor which you have chosen and in which you will be able to LEAD. There strives within you now a pulsating desire to attain. You are driven by a force that does not allow complications and interruptions to be taken as an every day part of life and therefore will not accept these as you are ever looking toward that time when these complications will not be a part of your life; however, realize that they do serve their purpose. They are not intended to be accepted as a part of living that is to be accepted and expected because in that way they would not be looked upon nor considered to be an inconvenience. They must not be accepted because they are inconveniences that must come to fulfill a passage of time that allows certain instances to result as a matter of process of going through/enduring complications.

People tend to pull/extract from you the very essence of your being therefore you are apt to share a part of yourself with those with whom you come in contact and therefore you have a great opportunity to exercise your abilities to be able to achieve insurmountable possibilities in that you can exercise your ability to allow yourself to become a part of that person's understanding to allow you to project yourself into the depths of their experience so that you might show them a way that is clear and precise.

Proceed in the manner in which you have been successful thus far and you will see that you have been instrumental in bringing and drawing many souls from here and there to a deeper meaning of life and what it holds by way of commanding ones self to a point where life can bear much influence when used and directed by that which causes turning points to be deciding factors as to the outcome of existence.

Success means to succeed at a given chore. Your purpose has been outlined before and therefore success will come as a matter of completing that which has been given you to do. Methods to achieve are daily being enlightened in your thoughts and your movements are guided so that your success is assured. Many times you have been given thoughts that have allowed you to see the true purpose for what has been spoken and enlightenment of your thoughts in this manner has allowed you to achieve in ways that you may not have been aware. There happens to be a matter that will be straightened so that you may make progress at a more rapid pace. Energy required to maintain your ability to retain all that which is coming your way and is a part of you already is great. Allow this to be your refuge in a time when you are despairing of trying to receive, that energy must be allowed to generate itself within your being as you require much to allow that which exerts itself from your being to go forward.

Proceed and attract that which is being sent your way by the very act of persevering and knowing it will come. True discipleship is the ability to go forward on the basis that what you believe in is true and real and what has been promised will be delivered at the proper time and by the means which is fitting the occasion. This must not be looked upon as a shallow promise as any promise that is given by God holds much as far as fulfillment and achievement of purpose is concerned. It will avail much and one day the benefits derived from patience extolled upon your part will well exceed what went into making it so.

This has been very little in the way of instruction, however, much that has been planned for you is on a course that is being completed but cannot be forthcoming until complications spoken of before have made the way clear so that you might walk freely knowing that burdens lifted have enabled you to fully realize the filling of energy and put to proper use that which is constantly being renewed so that you might reach out and do that which is required of you to do with ease of mind and body. Control and be directive in your ways. Deciding factors will present themselves. Your state of mind will enable you to proceed at that rate which is acceptable to you. You are under great stress at this time but this too will pass. Being what you are requires much but you will see that all is not in vain if done in the proper spirit and you have the proper spirit but you need encouragement that will soon be forthcoming and will enable you to be that which you are.

Blessing your efforts as always,
Signature Blurred

As 1977 comes to a close and the holidays and family obligations present themselves Wilma is joyous and amazed at the body of material that has been received in just over these last five months. Her enthusiasm in receiving this material has not diminished and she looks forward to these sessions with anticipation and excitement. She does not know how long these sessions will continue but she is willing to receive as long as these spirit teachers/angels are willing to present this information.

What a privilege Wilma feels to be in a position to receive these messages and teachings dictated from spirit teachers/angels from the other side. Wilma is excited for the New Year to begin to see what new information will be revealed.

Dictated messages and teachings continue to be received through

Wilma Jean Jones in:

An Angel Told Me So

Volume Two

Visit Michael's website at spiritspeaks.com to view Wilma Jean Jones television interview. Also available is one of Michael's articles that has been posted to the Edgar Cayce blog. This blog is posted by the Edgar Cayce foundation, the Association of Research and Enlightenment, headquartered in Virginia Beach, Virginia.

Michael also offers a set of his own writings

Spiritual Parchment Prints

Available on his website.

Notes

Notes

Notes

Notes